D0309988

Modelling
and simulation

J.R. Leigh

PETER PEREGRINUS LTD
on behalf of the
Institution of Electrical Engineers

Published by Peter Peregrinus Ltd., London, UK.

©1983: Peter Peregrinus Ltd

British Library Cataloguing in Publication Data

Leigh, J.R.
    Modelling and simulation.—(IEE topics in
    control series; 1)
    1. Mathematical models
    I. Title   II. Series
    511',8   QA401

ISBN 0-906048-95-8

Printed in England by Short Run Press Ltd., Exeter

IEE TOPICS IN CONTROL SERIES 1
Series Editors: Prof. B.H. Swanick
Prof. H. Nicholson

Modelling and simulation

Preface

These notes are based on lectures in Modelling and Simulation given to the MSc course in Instrumentation and Digital Systems at the Polytechnic of Central London. The Polytechnic course includes practical sessions involving the use of simulation languages. I have not thought it worthwhile to describe these aspects since each lecturer will use different local simulation facilities. The material in these notes can be covered in about 24 hours. For many purposes, a treatment excluding Chapters 10 and 11 will be adequate, allowing a corresponding time saving.

Contents

Introduction and overview

Mathematical models are finding increasing application in a variety of fields. These notes are written primarily to cover the construction, testing and use of models for engineering applications. However, the techniques described are applicable to any situation for which causal equations can be written and/or where input–output data can be obtained.

Considering the engineering field, the use of models can be divided into two main categories:

(*a*) models to assist engineering design;
(*b*) models for use in control system design or for inclusion within control systems.

A brief discussion on types of models, particularly those in category (*b*), is given in Chapter 1.

Chapter 2 reviews the modelling of single-input–single-output linear systems from a slightly novel viewpoint, chosen so that the results can fit easily into the context of the other chapters.

The central theme of these notes — the modelling and simulation of relatively complex systems begins in Chapter 3 with the establishment of a methodology for the construction of models.

Most dynamic models are constructed around a set of differential equations. Accordingly, Chapter 4 is concerned with differential equations and their solution in the digital computer.

The main theme of these notes is concluded by chapters on parameter estimation, linearisation and model reduction techniques.

Chapters 10 and 11 are mathematically more demanding than the earlier chapters and are designed to give a taste of how functional analysis can be applied with advantage to infinite dimensional problems.

The words modelling, identification and simulation appear frequently in the notes. Accordingly it is useful to define these words: A *mathematical model* is 'a mathematical representation of the significant, relevant aspects of an existing or proposed physical system'. (Significance and relevance being in relation to an application where the model is to be used.)

Identification is defined, following Zadeh, as 'the determination on the basis of input and output of a system, within a specified class of systems, to which the system under test is equivalent'.

Simulation is 'the setting up of a computational analogue of a physical system'.

Chapter 1

Types of models

1.0 Classification of models

Models can be classified according to purpose. In the first category are *models to assist plant design and operation*. The second category consists of *models to assist control system design and operation*.

1.0.1 Models to assist plant design and operation

(*a*) Detailed, physically based, often non-dynamic models to assist in fixing plant dimensions and other basic parameters.
(*b*) Economic models allowing the size and product mix of a projected plant to be selected.
(*c*) Economic models to assist decisions on plant modernisation.

For process design purposes, a model can usually be non-dynamic but it must operate at high accuracy over a wide range. The accuracy requirement means that many detailed second order effects have to be included while the wide range requirement means that non-linearities need to be carefully modelled.

1.0.2 Models to assist control system design and operation

(*a*) Fairly complete dynamic models, valid over a wide range of process operation to assist detailed quantitative design of a control system.
(*b*) Simple models based on crude approximation to the plant, but including some economically quantifiable variables, to allow the scope and type of a proposed control system to be decided.
(*c*) Reduced dynamic models for use on-line as part of a control system. Models for control purposes do not in general need to operate over a wide range and hence they can often be linearised models. A sufficient accuracy can often be achieved by numerical fitting of the model to be observed data and this allows effects of small significance to be neglected. However, the model for control purposes will always be a dynamic model.

Some types of control system require an *on-line predictive model*. Such a model introduces special problems in that future values of the uncontrolled plant inputs are not available and estimates must be used. To illustrate this, suppose that a plant using a varying raw material is to be controlled using a predictive model. Assumptions must be made about the composition of the future raw material in order for the predictive model to operate.

Where the model is to be used to assist in the design of an optimal controller a model must be produced that is mathematically tractable. In particular, it will be advantageous if the principal equations are differentiable.

It should be noted that there exist methods for carrying out plant optimisation on-line without the use of a model. The performance of the plant is measured and by a succession of controlled perturbations, the operating point of the plant is moved to maximise the performance. This approach has

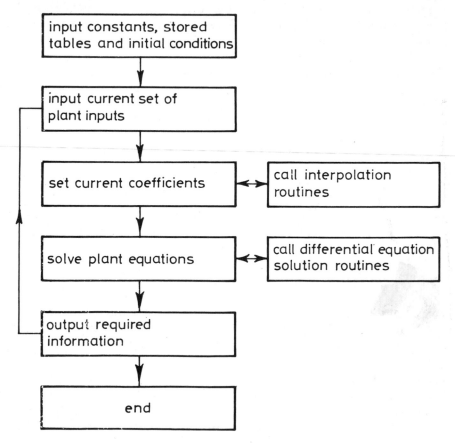

Fig. 1.1 *Flow diagram of the computer program for a typical mathematical model*

been called evolutionary operation. It is applicable to continuous plants whose condition changes only slowly with time.

Because of the different nature of the models for design and control, it is in practice very difficult to derive one from the other. Sometimes a design model has been used to generate tables of 'bench mark' steady state conditions and a dynamic model has been made to operate about each steady state. However, in general it is difficult to integrate satisfactorily the two models into a dual purpose model.

The *extent of use* of a model will affect its complexity. A model that must represent a range of types of plant and a range of sizes of plant must necessarily be more complex than a model that has to represent a single plant. In particular, the single plant model can include empirical equations that are valid only for that plant while a further simplification is that plant dependent coefficients can be regarded as constant.

The information from which a mathematical model is built includes material flow diagrams, block diagrams, circuit diagrams, algebraic and differential equations and curves and tables. To this must be added the results of experiments and data logging trials. The resulting mathematical model is assembled into a computer program. The flow diagram for the computer program of a typical mathematical model is shown in Fig. 1.1.

1.1 Some examples of the use of models in control systems applications

The greatest use of models is undoubtedly in simulation. This type of use is easily visualised — a planned set of experiments is carried out on the model rather than in the real-life situation. Simulation will be undertaken whenever it is cheaper, quicker or safer than the real-life alternative or (as in forecasting) when the real-life alternative does not exist.

In control systems applications, models are used on-line in a number of interesting ways. Examples are given below.

1.1.1 Use of models on-line in an advisory mode

Steel ingot heating model: Steel is cast into batches of ingots each of about 10 tonnes weight. When the ingots are removed from their moulds the exterior of the ingot is at a relatively low temperature while the interior is very hot and may still be molten. Before the ingots can be reduced in size by rolling, the temperature must be reasonably uniform throughout. To achieve this, the ingots are transferred to heated furnaces called soaking pits where they remain until ready to roll. The factors that determine the temperature distribution in an ingot include its dimensions, its history of casting and stripping and the heating conditions in the soaking pit. A statistical or deterministic model can advise the operator when any particular batch of ingots will be ready to roll.

Since in a typical works, there may be 20 soaking pits each holding 20 ingots there is also a difficult scheduling problem to obtain good plant utilisation. The heating model can form a key part of an overall computer assisted scheduling system of the soaking pit area.

Petrochemical plant control: A large model-based advisory control scheme[1] has been developed by the petrochemical industry. This system, which involves an inter-connected set of complementary models, produces operator advice aimed at moving towards and maintaining optimum overall operation.

1.1.2 Use of a model as part of an on-line control scheme

To overcome a finite delay in the control loop due to a measurement siting problem: The first Fig. 1.2 shows a control system for maintaining correct diameter in an extrusion plant when insulation is added to electric cables.

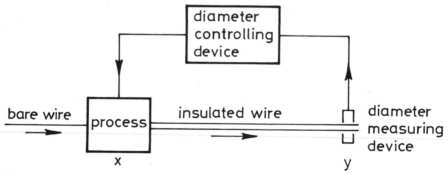

Fig. 1.2   *Control of cable diameter in the presence of measurement delay*

For physical reasons, the cable diameter cannot be measured until the point *y*. This leads to a finite delay due to the transport time of the cable between *x* and *y*, and consequent severe limitation on the performance of the control scheme.

Figure 1.3 shows the use of an on-line model to overcome the problem. The model makes available, nearly instantaneously, an estimate of the output diameter and allows feed back control with the computation time now replacing the transport delay.

Note that the model still receives a measurement (shown dotted) of the cable diameter. This means that the model is in reality only required to estimate local fast variations about a measured mean diameter.

In a predictive-iterative control loop: A single on-line model is used in two different modes and the operation is best understood by considering separate diagrams for the two modes.

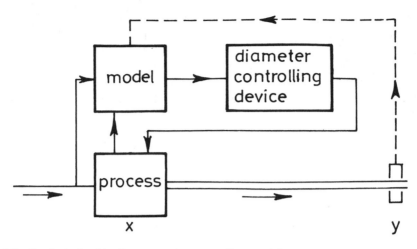

Fig. 1.3 *Control of cable diameter using an on-line model*

In the parallel mode (Fig. 1.4), the process model is updated to behave as closely as possible to the process as measured by the error criterion.

In the predictive mode (Fig. 1.5), the model operates iteratively in fast time, taking in trial control commands and predicting process outputs. When a satisfactory future performance has been predicted, the trial command is taken to be the new actual command over the next control period.

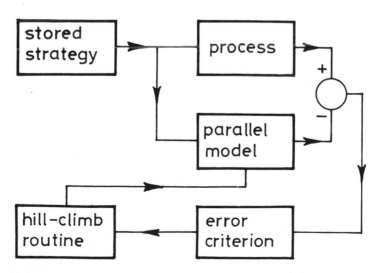

Fig. 1.4 *Parallel mode*

An interesting application of this approach was undertaken on blast furnaces of British Steel Corporation in South Wales. Further details can be found in Reference 2.

Other applications of mathematical models in on-line control are in model reference adaptive schemes and in Kalman filtering. References 3 and 5 describe the principles of these methods.

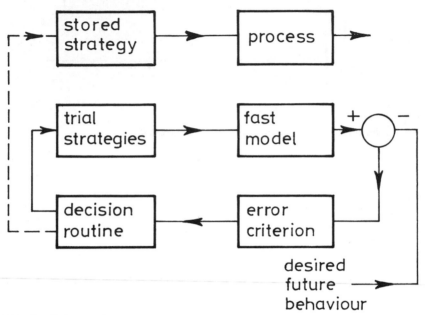

Fig. 1.5   *Predictive mode*

1.2 References

1 ROBINS, T.: 'Computer control at the B.P. Baglan Bay Plant', *Anglo–Soviet Colloquium on Instrumentation in the Petrochemical Industry*, Polytechnic of Central London, 1976.

2. WOOD, B. I.: 'Simulation and control of the blast furnace process', *Proc. 5th UKAC Convention*, University of Bath, 1973.

3 KALMAN, R. E.: 'A new approach to linear filtering and prediction problems', *Trans. ASME J. Basic Eng.*, 1960, **82**, pp. 35–45.

4 KALMAN, R. E. and BUCY, R. S.: 'New results in linear filtering and prediction theory', *Trans. ASME J. Basic Eng.*, 1961, **83**, pp. 95–108.

5 LANDAU, I. D.: 'A survey of model reference adaptive techniques, theory and applications', *Automatica*, 1974, **10**, pp. 353–379.

Chapter 2

The modelling of single-input–single-output systems

2.0 Introduction

Single-input–single-output systems occur as sub-systems embedded in larger systems. Often it will be desirable to study a particular sub-system in detail because it plays a key role in determining overall system performance.

Modelling of simple systems can often be undertaken successfully using quite elementary techniques.

The section that follows considers four possible domains of representation for single-input–single-output systems.

2.1 Domains of representation

2.1.1 Time domain (A)
Experimental data occur initially only in the time domain. Where a single-input–single-output system is being modelled it will often be possible to apply deterministic signals and to record, for example, *step, ramp or sinusoidal responses* in a relatively noise free situation. Such tests will often also be valuable in the preliminary study of isolated systems with non-linearities.

2.1.2 Frequency domain (B)
In the above simple situation it will usually be possible to use a transfer function analyser to produce *frequency response* information equivalent to the time domain information.

Where the system to be modelled must be tested while it remains operational, the preferred method of experimentation could be by injection of pseudo-random binary signals, of a magnitude insufficient to be detrimental to the system operation, followed by *cross-correlation*, either in real time or on recorded input–output data. By Fourier transforming the cross-correlation function, the frequency response of the system under test can be obtained.

The time domain responses, frequency responses and cross-correlation functions can themselves be considered as models or representations of the systems from which they arise.

It should be noted that such models contain no assumptions, parameters or structure inserted by the modeller. They are in a sense, implicit models and usually they need to be transformed to a different representation before they can be usefully applied.

Transformations considered here are into the pole-zero domain or the state space domain.

2.1.3 Pole zero domain representation (C)

For a single input single output system the pole zero model is the transfer function

$$G(s) = \frac{a_n s + \ldots + a_1 s + a_0}{b s^n + - \ldots + b_1 s + b_0} \tag{2.1.1}$$

where the poles and zeroes are the roots of the denominator and numerator respectively.

This representation contains specific parameters and an assumption about the order of the system. Therefore, in moving from representations A, B to this representation, the system order needs to be estimated either from physical reasoning, by examination of the structure of the system being modelled, or by a numerical method. Given the system order, the parameters a_i, b_i of eqn. (2.1.1) still need to be allocated numerical values. The problems of determining system order and parameters are discussed in later sections.

2.1.4 State space domain (D)

The general state space representation is

$$\left.\begin{array}{l} \dot{x} = Ax + Bu \\ y = Cx + Du \end{array}\right\}, \tag{2.1.2}$$

where x, u, y are the state, input and output vectors respectively of dimensions n, r, m. A, B, C, D are constant matrices.

Since this section is concerned with single-input–single-output systems, $r = m = 1$ but n, the system order, is to be determined as for representation C. Further structure is present in this representation since:

(a) This model, unlike that of C, is expected to operate with non-zero initial conditions.

(b) A suitable set of state variables has to be chosen. Where physical knowledge of the component structure is available, one method of choosing state variables is to draw an analogue simulation of the system, and to take the output of every integrator as a state variable. This method and alternatives are explained in detail in Reference 1, Chapter 3.

Figure 2.1 illustrates the main features of this section.

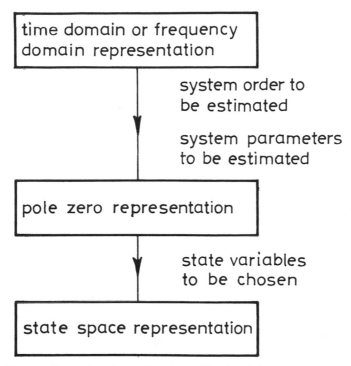

Fig. 2.1   *Diagram illustrating the main points of Section 2.1*

2.2 Determination of the order of a system from input/output data

If additional parameters are added to a model, the error between model and process can be expected always to decrease.

The basis for deciding when a model has reached a sufficiently high order must always be statistical.

In statistically based models formed from input/output data (regression models, least squares models, etc.), significance tests can be used to decide on a satisfactory order for a model.

For physically based models, the best basis for including or rejecting additional parameters is the consistency of the parameter set. The principle is that if additional redundant parameters are added that interact with the existing parameter set then, over many data runs, the augmented parameter set will show inconsistency. A method described in Reference 2, using this principle, requires the input of a standard set of k different inputs, say $\{u_j(t)\}$ $i = 1, ..., k$, to models $M_0, M_1, M_2,...$ of increasing order or structure.

For each of the k data inputs to the model M_0 the parameters a_{0ij} of the model are determined (where the meaning of the suffices is given below).

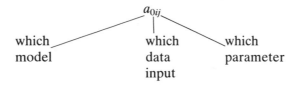

which model   which data input   which parameter

Over the runs $i = 1, ..., k$, the variance of each parameter is calculated, i.e., σ_{0j}^2 is calculated for each parameter, where

$$\sigma_{0j}^2 = \frac{1}{k-1} \sum_{i=1}^{k} (a_{0ij} - \overline{a_{0ij}})^2.$$

This procedure is repeated for the models $M_1, M_2, ...$ of increasing order or structure to yield a table as follows:

Model	*Variance of individual parameters*			Criterion
	a_1	a_2	a_3	
M_0				C_0
M_1				C_1
M_2				C_2

In the final 'criterion column' the variance of the individual variances appears. This is defined by

$$C = \text{var} (\text{var } a_j), \quad j = 1, ..., l,$$

where l is the number of parameters, which of course varies according to the row of the table.

The disadvantage of this approach is the amount of computation required, since each row in the table requires the estimation of $l \times k$ parameters. k needs to be reasonably large, say $k_{\min} = 50$ to allow the method to be reliable and the time requirement may therefore be excessive.

2.3 Determination of system parameters (Based on Chidambara[3]. See also Raven[4], for another method)

Let a linear system of order n be written in the canonical form

$$\begin{pmatrix} \dot{x}_1 \\ \dot{x}_2 \\ \vdots \\ \dot{x}_n \end{pmatrix} = \begin{pmatrix} -a_1 & -a_2 & \cdots & \cdot & -a_n \\ 1 & 0 & \cdots & \cdot & 0 \\ 0 & 1 & \cdots & \cdot & 0 \\ \cdot & \cdot & \cdots & \cdot & \cdot \\ 0 & 0 & \cdots & 1 & 0 \end{pmatrix} \begin{pmatrix} x_1 \\ x_2 \\ \vdots \\ x_n \end{pmatrix} + \begin{pmatrix} b_1 \\ b_2 \\ \vdots \\ b_n \end{pmatrix} u,$$

Let $y = -ax$,   (2.3.1)

where $a = (a_1, a_2, \ldots, a_n)$.

Eqn. (2.3.1) can be written in the alternative form

$$\dot{x} = Jx + bu + fy$$ (2.3.2)

where

$$J = \begin{pmatrix} 0 & 0 & \cdots & 0 & 0 \\ 1 & 0 & \cdots & 0 & 0 \\ 0 & 1 & \cdots & 0 & 0 \\ \cdot & \cdot & \cdots & \cdot & \cdot \\ 0 & 0 & \cdots & 1 & 0 \end{pmatrix}, \quad f = \begin{pmatrix} 1 \\ 0 \\ \cdot \\ 0 \end{pmatrix}, \quad b = \begin{pmatrix} b_1 \\ b_2 \\ \cdot \\ b_n \end{pmatrix}$$

2.3.1 Determination of the b parameters

from eqn. (2.3.2),

$$\dot{x}_1 = y + b_1 u.$$

Assume that $u(t)$ is a unit step input and that the steady-state value of y is available, then

$$b_1 = y(t), \qquad t \to \infty.$$

The remaining b values are obtained from the equation

$$b_i = -\int_0^t (y(\tau) + b_{i-1}(\tau)) \, d\tau, \quad i = 2, \ldots, n, \quad t \to \infty.$$

The procedure also generates the state variables, since

$$x_1(t) = \int_0^t (y(\tau) + b_1 u(\tau)) \, d\tau,$$

$$x_i(t) = \int_0^t (x_{i-1}(\tau) + b_i u(\tau)) \, d\tau, \quad i = 2, \ldots, n.$$

2.3.2 Determination of the a parameters

$$y(t) = -ax(t).$$

Define

$$\tilde{y}(t) = y(t) - y(t) \underset{t \to \infty}{,}$$

$$\tilde{x}(t) = x(t) - x(t) \underset{t \to \infty}{,}$$

Then

$$\bar{y}(t) = - a\bar{x}(t).$$

Multiply both sides by $\bar{x}(t)^T$ and integrate to yield, after a little manipulation,

$$a = \left(\int_0^t \bar{y}(\tau)\bar{x}^T(\tau) \ d\tau \right)\left(\int_0^t \bar{x}(\tau)\bar{x}^T(\tau) \ d\tau \right)^{-1}.$$

For the determination of the vector a, any convenient value of t can be used.

2.4 References

1 TOU, J. T.: *Modern Control Theory*, McGraw-Hill, New York (1964).
2 DESAI, V. K. and FAIRMAN, F. W.: 'On determining the order of a linear system', *Mathematical Biosciences*, 1971, **12**, pp. 217–224.
3 CHIDAMBARA, M. R.: 'A new canonical form of a state-variable equation and its application in the determination of a mathematical model of an unknown system', *Int. J. Control*, 1971, **14**, No. 5, pp. 897–909.
4 RAVEN, E. A.: 'A minimum realisation method', *IEEE Control Systems Magazine*, 1981, **1**, No. 3, pp. 14–20.

Chapter 3

Techniques for the modelling of more complex processes

3.0 A methodology for model building

The initial stage in model building is to assemble equations representing the physical mechanisms that are believed to be applicable to the plant. (This procedure is described in Section 3.1.) A selection from these equations is then manipulated to obtain a framework for the desired mathematical model.

The different types of information available to the model builder will often be incompatible, because they exist at different theoretical levels, and are impossible to combine. For instance, equations representing the basic process may well be extensive and complex, being based on a rather profound process theory. This gives rise to many internal relationships with unknown inaccessible parameters. At the other extreme there will be semi-empirical relationships with a small number of variables. Assuming that the equations can be made compatible, the next stage of equation selection can proceed. All equations that will have significant effect on the model behaviour must obviously be included. Equations whose effect is unknown can also be included at this point — they can be removed later if they have no part to play. The disadvantage of this strategy is that the initial model is likely to be large and complex and it may be difficult in practice to eliminate the redundant equations. The alternative, to produce first a simple model and to refine this until it performs as required, is in practice more attractive for most applications.

Unknown coefficients in the model equations are determined if possible from the process literature or from specially devised tests. They are stored either as numerical values or in look-up tables. The remaining unknown coefficients in the model must be determined by parameter estimation techniques as described in later chapters of these notes.

Plant data must be obtained for the purpose of parameter estimation and for model validation. Sufficient data must be available to allow statistically meaningful tests to be carried out and the data must span the range of conditions over which the model has to operate. Obtaining sufficient reliable data of the right type from a large industrial plant is a costly, time consuming exercise. There is a temptation to use normal operating records, but this can be done successfully only in a minority of cases. Usually, a specially conducted data collection trial is required involving augmented instrumentation, controlled plant conditions and specially injected disturbances. Where an existing plant is being modelled, it will usually be the intention to modify the plant, for instance by the application of an improved control system. Thus, the data collection trial must take the plant into regimes that are part of its expected future range of operation rather than its existing, perhaps more limited, range.

For plants not yet in existence, it may be possible to use data from an existing similar plant, although even nominally identical plants differ markedly in practice in their numerical coefficients. Difficult coefficients for plants not yet existing will have to be obtained from pilot plant or laboratory tests concentrated on this one aspect. For instance, wind tunnel tests on a perspex model may be used to obtain an aerodynamic coefficient. Such an approach can be used only when the model has a sound and well specified theoretical basis.

Once the best coefficient values have been obtained, the model is tested against plant data to determine whether it meets the modelling criterion laid down previously. Except for very simple plants, it is very unlikely that the modelling criterion will be satisfied at the first or second attempt. Model building is essentially interative as shown in Fig. 3.1.

3.0.1 Estimation of best possible model accuracy

During the stages of model refinement it is useful to have an estimate of the highest accuracy that can be expected from a perfect model, bearing in mind the statistical properties of the available input data. As an illustration, assume that a many-input–single-output model has the form $y = f(u_1, ..., u_r)$, where the inputs u_i are subject to independent random errors. Then the variance of the output of the model due to the errors in the inputs is given by

$$\sigma^2(y) = \sum_{i=1}^{r} \left(\frac{\partial f}{\partial u_i}\right)^2 \sigma^2(u_i). \tag{3.0.2}$$

An example given in reference 1 relates to the estimation of temperature in steel-making where an appropriate analysis of the type described above, showed that the variance of temperature predicted by the model should be around 10°C. Once accuracy of this order has been obtained, it is useless to seek further accuracy by model refinement. Any further improvement in accuracy must be sought by improving the accuracy of measurement or data processing.

3.0.2 Residual analysis

Residual analysis is concerned with the examination of plots of the error between model output and recorded plant output, against time or against some other variable. Any deterministic trend in such plots indicates the presence of an effect that has not been adequately modelled. Davidson[1], describes this procedure in detail.

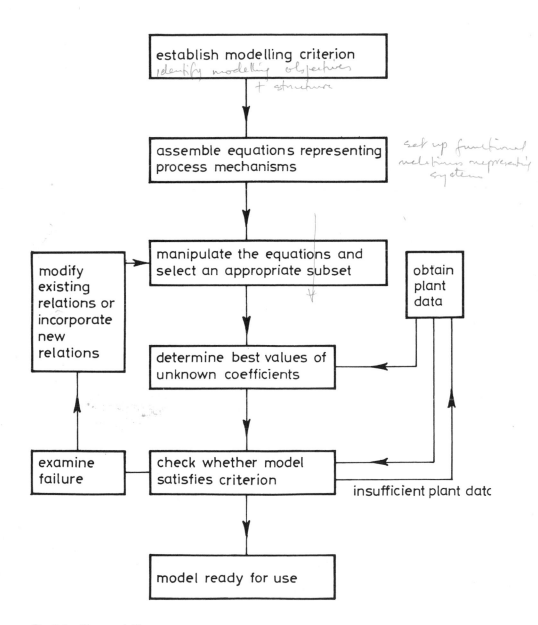

Fig. 3.1 *The modelling process*

3.1 Assembly of equations representing the basic plant mechanisms

The first stage in model building is to assemble equations representing all relevant mechanisms and components of the plant. Obviously, the equations will vary greatly according to the nature of the plant so that superficially there will appear to be little similarity between the equations representing different processes. However, in the initial search for basic equations the principles of *invariance* and *equilibrium* can be applied to the plant and to subsets of plant. For a plant producing a product, the invariance principle leads to a set of *mass balance equations* of the general form

$$\text{output mass } y = \text{input mass } u \pm \text{mass stored internally } q. \qquad (3.1.1)$$

For a real plant, the set of equations representing this mass balance will be quite complex. Obviously, eqn. (3.1.1) can be differentiated to produce relationships between flow rates,

$$\frac{dy}{dt} = \frac{du}{dt} \pm \frac{dq}{dt}. \qquad (3.1.2)$$

Other results of application of the principle of invariance are:

A thermal balance equation

$$\text{heat generated internally} = \text{sensible heat of products entering} -$$
$$\text{sensible heat of products leaving} \pm \text{heat}$$
$$\text{produced or absorbed by}$$
$$\text{process.} \qquad (3.1.3)$$

An energy balance equation

$$\text{energy in system at time } t = \text{energy in system at time } 0$$
$$\pm \text{ energy dissipated or fed into the}$$
$$\text{system in the interval } (0, t). \qquad (3.1.4)$$

A detailed balance of the energy in a system will often lead to a set of sound basic equations that can form the foundation for a model.

This is to be expected since most dynamic systems can be characterised by their energy storage and energy dissipation behaviour.

The equilibrium equations include *Newton's law* for mechanical systems:

$$\text{applied force} = \text{mass} \times \text{acceleration} - \text{friction force,} \qquad (3.1.5)$$

$$\text{applied torque} = \text{inertia} \times \text{angular acceleration} - \text{friction}$$
$$\text{torque,} \qquad (3.1.6)$$

while for electrical systems *Kirchhoff's laws* apply:

$$\text{the algebraic sum of currents at a node is zero,} \qquad (3.1.7)$$

$$\text{the sum of voltages around a closed circuit is zero.} \qquad (3.1.8)$$

The above relationships are of course very elementary but in a real situation there will be many such equations and the application of invariance and equilibrium principles leads to a structured approach to this initial stage of modelling. The initial equations will thus be the well known basic laws of physics and chemistry, particularly those related to invariance and equilibrium. For very simple plants, sufficient basic information may be generated by the above procedure to allow a model to be built. However, even for very simple plants there is usually at least one difficult relationship that cannot easily be represented. Two examples illustrate this point. Consider the steering of a ship. It will be relatively easy to model the behaviour of the internal mechanisms of the ship including the rudder dynamics. However, the effect on the ship's course of a change of rudder angle is obviously not so simple. At the very least it will depend on the speed and geometry of the ship. Consider next the simple case of a cold object suddenly inserted into a constant temperature oven held at 1000°C. Although the laws of heat radiation are directly applicable, the emissivity of the surface of the heated object is unlikely to be constant and will have to be determined experimentally.

The equations representing individual components of the plant will often be elementary and obvious. However, it is still useful to make use of a table of components and their analogues such as that given in Fig. 3.2.

Although the table and other elementary relations give a good foundation, a plant rarely satisfies the initial assumptions made at the start of the modelling procedure and the modelling of process imperfections, non-linearities, non-homogenity, etc., requires detailed process knowledge and experimentation.

As an illustration, consider the rolling of hot metal strip between a single pair of parallel rolls as shown in Fig. 3.3.

Let H, h be the input and output thickness respectively. Let θ be the temperature of the strip in the roll gap. Let R be the radius of the rolls and S the gap between the rolls when no strip is being rolled. Let ω be the angular velocity of the rolls, μ the coefficient of friction between the rolls and the strip, λ be a parameter representing the composition of material being rolled.

Let M be the stiffness of the housing supporting the rolls and F be the separating force between the rolls.

The following equations can be found in the literature on metal rolling.

$$F = f(H, h, \theta, R, \omega, \mu, \lambda) \quad \text{roll force equation.} \qquad (3.1.9)$$

$$h = S + F/M \qquad \text{Hooke's law.} \qquad (3.1.10)$$

These two equations can form the theoretical basis for a rolling model. However, even to satisfy relatively modest accuracy requirements, the following 'imperfections' must be taken into account.

	Generalised component	Electrical	Mechanical linear	Mechanical rotational	Thermal component	Hydraulic component	Pneumatic component
Resistive Component	$R = b/a$ Resistance	$R = v/i$ Resistance	$F = p/w$ Friction coefficient	$f = a/\omega$ Friction coefficient	$R = \theta/i$ Thermal resistance	$R = p/i$ Resistance	$R = p/i$ Resistance
Capacitive Component	$C = \frac{1}{a}\int b\, dt$ Capacitance	$C = \frac{1}{v}\int i\, dt$ Capacitance	$k = \frac{1}{p}\int w\, dt$ Spring constant	$k = \frac{1}{a}\int \omega\, dt$ Spring constant	$C = \frac{1}{\theta}\int i\, dt$ Thermal capacitance	$k = \frac{1}{p}\int i\, dt$ Compressibility	$k = \frac{1}{p}\int i\, dt$ Compressibility
Inertial Component	$J = a/(db/dt)$ Inertia	$L = v/(di/dt)$ Inductance	$M = p/(dw/dt)$ Mass	$J = a/(d\omega/dt)$ Inertia	Property does not exist	$J = p/(di/dt)$ Liquid inertia	$J = p/(di/dt)$ Gas inertia
Through variable	b	Current i	Velocity v	Angular ω	Heat flow i	Liquid flow i	Gas flow i
Across variable	a	Voltage v	Force p	Torque a	Temperature difference	Pressure drop p	Pressure drop p

Fig. 3.2 *Components and their analogues*

(a) The stiffness of the housing cannot be represented by a simple parameter M but rather by a curve that must be determined experimentally and stored.
(b) The rolls are no longer parallel when subjected to forces generated by rolling.
(c) The rolls are not perfectly circular due to wear and other imperfections.
(d) The rolls are flattened where in contact with the strip so that the value of R for substitution into the roll force equation is not that of the unloaded rolls.
(e) S is speed dependent because of oil film effects in the roll bearings.

In addition μ, θ and S, are very difficult to measure for input to the model.

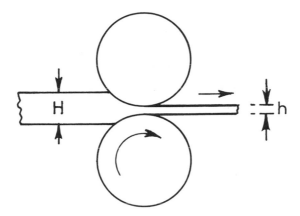

Fig. 3.3

In modelling, the stage of writing down meaningful equations, representing a particular physical situation, proceeds in a rather *ad hoc* manner guided by experience and intuition as well as by the physical laws. It has often been suggested that a more scientific procedure could be developed using a combination of network theory, block diagram algebra: conservation principles and thermodynamic principles. This is an area of current research and no method is yet available that offers advantages in general. However, it is useful for anyone working in the modelling field to be aware of developments in this area and a good overview can be obtained in Reference 2. One of the central themes to emerge from research in this area is the *bond graph*. For an introduction to this approach References 3 and 4 can be consulted.

3.2 Constants, coefficients and variables

The model may contain one or more true constants, e.g., Planck's constant or the mechanical equivalent of heat. Such constants obviously present no problems. Other coefficients may be approximately *constant over the whole range of operation* of the model and for practical purposes they can also be regarded as constant. Examples are ambient temperature and physical dimensions of the plant.

Some coefficients may be *considered constant during any particular run of the model*. For instance in a batch process, certain coefficients will be constant for the duration of the batch but need resetting for each subsequent batch. In a continuous process, raw material density and composition can perhaps be considered constant during the lifetime of a particular consignment of raw material. When a new consignment of raw material comes into use, the appropriate coefficients must be modified. The discontinuity in the coefficient values causes a process disturbance that may have to be evaluated quantitatively by the model.

Finally, there are *coefficients that need to be modified during the running* of the model. Current values are determined either from a stored formula or by interpolation in the stored table. Examples are load torque as a function of speed and the inductance of an iron cored coil as a function of current in the coil.

A dynamic model in the form of a vector-matrix differential equation

$$\dot{x} = Ax + Bu,$$
$$y = Cx, \tag{3.2.1}$$

has a natural classification of variables.

x is an n-dimensional vector of *state variables* where n is the order of the system.

y is an m-dimensional vector of *output variables*. In practice each of the elements of y must be determined by observation or measurement.

u is an r-dimensional vector of *input variables*. This vector must contain elements representing changing plant inputs, all known external disturbances that are to be represented and the control variables.

An advantage of the vector-matrix formulation is that it leads naturally to a systematic classification of variables. Even if the model is not in a vector-matrix form, a similiar type of classification of variables is still possible and desirable.

3.2.1 Coefficient invariance
If a model contains redundant variables or highly correlated variables then large changes can be made in some coefficient values without significantly altering the behaviour of the model. i.e., a wide range of coefficient values give the same performance from the model. In this situation small changes in the plant give rise to large changes in the coefficients of the model. A model of a time invariant plant should not change its coefficients greatly, when fitted against different sets of plant data. Any significant change should be investigated and redundant variables and strong correlations between variables eliminated.

3.3 Definitions of error between model and process

This section is based on reference 1.

(*a*) The usual definition of error is *output error* defined as

$$e_0 = y - \hat{y} = y - M(u).$$

The notation $M(u)$ denoting that for a particular model, the output y is a function of u. (See Fig. 3.4.)

(*b*) *Input error* is defined by

$$e_i = u - \hat{u} = u - M^{-1}(y).$$

(See Fig. 3.5.)

(*c*) *Generalised error* is defined as

$$e_g = M_2^{-1}(y) - M_1(u).$$

(See Fig. 3.6.)

It is shown in Reference 5 how the proper choice of an error criterion can lead to linearity in the parameters so that the parameter estimation problem can be dealt with by linear methods.

3.4 Reasons for model failure

Even after considerable expenditure of effort, it happens that a model may not meet the specification laid down for it. Failure can occur due to:

(*a*) lack of sufficient relevant plant data with which to develop the model;

(*b*) failure to obtain a well structured foundation to support the latter stages of model refinement — this is due to lack of expertise or lack of process knowledge;

(*c*) numerical or computational problems of model implementation including — failure of convergence of iterative loops, and

— excessive time requirements of computation so that the model is virtually useless.

3.4.1 Failure of convergence of iterative loops

The principle is as follows. Two equations that are too complex to be combined are solved separately successively to yield an iterative process. Let the two equations be:

(*a*) $y = mx + c,$

(*b*) $y = lx + d$ or $x = l^{-1}(y - d).$

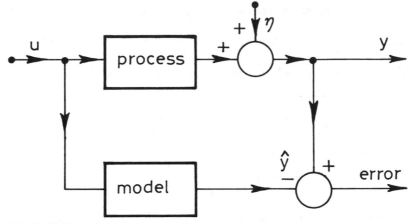

Fig. 3.4   *Definition of output error*

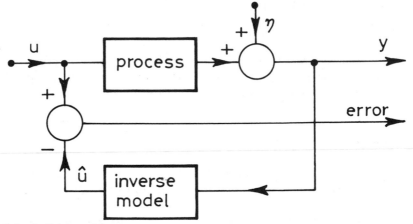

Fig. 3.5   *Definition of input error*

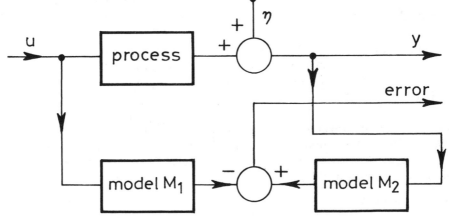

Fig. 3.6   *Definition of generalised error*

An initial estimate x_0 is inserted into eqn. (a) leading to an estimate $y_0 \cdot y_0$ inserted into eqn. (b) produces an estimate x_1, which, inserted into equation (a) produces an estimate y_1. This procedure is continued until x_n, y_n both satisfy the equation as closely as desired. The procedure can be illustrated graphically as in Fig. 3.7.

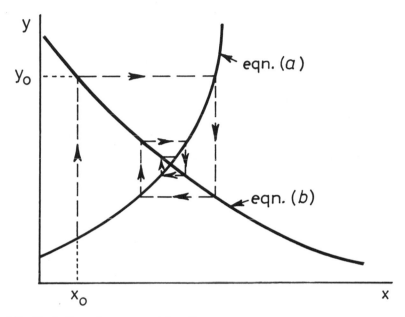

Fig. 3.7 *Illustration of convergent iteration*

The convergence of this and other iterative processes is best studied not by graphical methods but using the fixed point theorem as described below. Let an iterative process be represented in general by the relation

$$x_{n+1} = Ax_n, \tag{3.4.1}$$

where the operator A represents the iteration process and where x may be a vector. A is defined to be a *contraction operator* if

$$\|Ax\| < k\|x\| \quad \text{where } k \text{ satisfies } k < 1. \tag{3.4.2}$$

In case x is a scalar variable, A is defined to be a contraction operator if

$$|Ax| < k|x| \quad \text{where } k \text{ satisfies } k < 1.$$

3.4.2 Fixed point theorem
Let A be a contraction mapping and further let A satisfy the condition

$$\|Ax_1 - Ax_2\| < M\|x_1 - x_2\| \tag{3.4.3}$$

for some positive constant M and for any x_1, x_2. Then the recursive equation $x_{n+1} = Ax_n$ is convergent to a unique element x.

Example: Let the following equations be solved recursively using Newton's method.

$$y = a \ln (x) \quad \text{let } F = a \ln (x) - kx \text{ then } F = 0,$$

$$y = kx \qquad \text{implies that } x \text{ satisfies both equations.}$$

Newton's method leads to the recursive equation

$$x_{n+1} = x_n - F_n/F_n' \quad \text{where } F_n' = \frac{d}{dx}(F_n).$$

The convergence of this relation can be studied using the fixed point theorem. The interation process can be put in the form

$$x_{n+1} = Ax_n,$$

where

$$Ax_n = x_n - \frac{a \ln (x_n) - kx_n}{a/x_n - k} .$$

If A is a contraction operator the iteration procedure will converge to a unique x. By substituting in the values for a, k, and considering the range within which the values of x must lie, information on the convergence properties can be obtained.

3.5 References

1 DAVIDSON, H.: 'Statistical methods for model development', in book *Computer Control of Industrial Processes* (Edited by SAVAS, E. M.), McGraw-Hill, New York, 1965.
2 VAN DIXHOORN, J. J. and EVANS, F. J. (eds.): *Physical Structure in Systems Theory*, Academic Press, New York, 1974.
3 KARNOPP, D. and ROSENBERG, R.: *System Dynamics — a Unified Approach*, Wiley Interscience, New York, 1975.
4 THOMA, J.: *Introduction to Bond Graphs and Their Application*, Pergamon Press, New York, 1975.
5 ÅSTROM, K. J. and EYKHOFF, P.: 'System identification — a survey', *Automatica*, 1971, **1**, pp. 123–162.

Chapter 4

Ordinary differential equations and their solution in the digital computer

4.0 Introduction

Differential equations form the nucleus of most mathematical models. This chapter is mostly concerned with their solution. However it is suggested that wider reading on the subject of differential equations would be an advantage. Topics for reading might be existence, uniqueness, stability, behaviour at singularities and phase plane sketching. References 1 and 2 contain a wealth of suitable material.

4.1 Conditions for a mathematical model of a linear dynamic system to be well posed

A differential equation is said to be *well-posed* if:

(*a*) A solution to the equation *exists*.
(*b*) The solution is *unique*.
(*c*) The solution depends continuously on the *initial conditions*.

For a general non-linear differential equation the field is so broad that it is difficult to carry the discussion further. However, if we limit the discussion to sets of linear differential equations the situation is much simpler.

A linear dynamic system Σ can be defined axiomatically

$$\Sigma = \{I, U, X, \phi\},$$

where

I is an interval in the real line representing time,
U, X are normed linear spaces of functions on I,
U is the space of input functions assumed at least piece-wise continuous,
X is the state space,

φ is the transition mapping,

$$\phi: \quad X \times U \times I \rightarrow X,$$

φ is linear in the first two variables.

4.1.1 Axioms and consequential relations

(1) $\phi(x(t_0), t_0, u(t), t_1) = x(t_1)$,
$t_0, t, t_1 \; \varepsilon \; I, \quad x \; \varepsilon \; X, \quad u \; \varepsilon \; U$,

(2) $\phi(x(t_0), t_0, u(t), t) = \phi(0, t_0, u(t), t) + \phi(x(t_0, t_0, 0, t)$,

(3) $\phi(x(t_0), t_0, u(t), t_2) = \phi(\phi(x(t_0), t_0, u(t), t_1), t_1, u(t), t_2)$,

(4) $\phi(x(t_0), t_0, u_1(t), t) = \phi(x(t_0), t_0, u_2(t), t); \quad t_0, t \; \varepsilon \; T \subset I$,
$u_1(t) = u_2(t), \quad t \; \varepsilon \; T$,
$u_1(t) \neq u_2(t), \quad \text{otherwise.}$

Axiom (1) is the *equation solution property.*
Axiom (2) is a *decomposition property* dependent on the linearity of φ,
Axiom (3) is the *semi-group property.* It is clearly a necessary condition for uniqueness
Axiom (4) is the *causality condition.*
If the system Σ satisfies the further axiom (5) then Σ is said to be *time invariant.*

(5) $\phi(x(t_0), t_0, u(t_1), t_1) = \phi(x(t_0), t_0 + \tau, u(t), t_1 + \tau)$;
$t_0, t_1, \tau \; \varepsilon \; I.$

For further background on axiomatics, see Leigh.[3]

4.2 Linear differential equations — the time invariant case

Since every *n*th order differential equation can be represented equivalently by · *n* first order equations, it is convenient to consider such a set of first order equations.

$$\dot{x}_i(t) = \sum_{j=1}^{n} a_j x_j(t) + \sum_{j=1}^{r} b_j u_j(t); \quad i = 1, ..., n, \tag{4.2.1}$$

or in vector matrix notation, with *x*, *u* being vectors and *A*, *B* being matrices of coefficients

$$\dot{x}(t) = Ax(t) + Bu(t). \tag{4.2.2}$$

The solution of eqn. (4.22) can be written in the form

$$\dot{x}(t) = \Phi(t) x(0) + \int_0^t \Phi(t - \tau) Bu(\tau) \, d\tau \tag{4.2.3}$$

where $\Phi(t)$ is the *transition matrix*, $x(0)$ is the initial state, and τ is a dummy variable.

4.2.1 Numerical solution of eqn. (4.22)

First consider the solution with $u(t) \equiv 0$. Referring to axiom (3) in Section 4.1 above, it is clear that Φ satisfies the relation

$$\Phi(2t) = \Phi(t)\Phi(t). \tag{4.2.4}$$

For numerical solution we choose a small time step, T, calculate $\Phi(T)$ and generate a discrete representation $x(T)$, $x(2T)$, ..., $x(kT)$, ... of the continuous solution. All that is necessary is to have a sufficiently accurate representation for $\Phi(T)$.

In the general case with the forcing term $u(t)$ present, the right-hand integral term of eqn. (4.2.3) can, of course, be solved numerically but this is time consuming and usually it is possible to proceed as follows.

Choose a time step T sufficiently short that over every T, $u(t)$ can be considered constant, then eqn. (4.2.3) can be integrated to yield

$$x(T) = \Phi(T)x(0) - A^{-1}\Phi(T-\tau)Bu(0)|_0^T, \tag{4.2.5}$$

$$x(T) = \Phi(T)x(0) + A^{-1}[\Phi(T) - I]Bu(0), \tag{4.2.6}$$

which can be written

$$x(T) = \Phi(T)x(0) + \Psi(T)u(0), \tag{4.2.7}$$

where the matrix Ψ is defined by eqn. (4.2.6) provided that the matrix A is nonsingular.

Clearly, if the matrix Φ can be determined accurately by a computationally efficient method, the solution of sets of linear differential equations can be mechanised without difficulty. Accordingly, attention is devoted next to the determination of the transition matrix.

4.3 Methods of calculating the transition matrix

4.3.1 Series summation method

$\Phi(t)$ can be defined

$$\Phi(t) = e^{At} = I + At + \frac{A^2t^2}{2} + ...,$$

where I is the identity matrix.

This series can be shown to be always convergent and it is easily mechanised. However, convergence is in practice poor unless small values of t are chosen. This is usually the preferred method, with translation of t.

4.3.2 Laplace transform methods
Laplace transforming equation with $u(t) \equiv 0$ yields

$$sX(s) - x(0) = AX(s)$$

(Here, and only on this occasion, the capital letter X denotes a transformed variable), and inverse transforming

$$x(t) = L^{-1}\{(sI - A)^{-1}\}x(0), \quad \text{hence } \Phi(t) = L^{-1}\{(sI - A)^{-1}\}. \quad (4.3.1)$$

s is the complex Laplace variable and L^{-1} indicates inverse Laplace transformation.

4.3.3 Sylvester method
Provided that A has distinct eigenvalues, $\Phi(t)$ can be determined from the formula

$$\Phi(t) = \sum_{i=1}^{n} e^{\lambda_i t} \, F(\lambda_i), \quad (4.3.2)$$

where n is the order of the matrix A, and λ_i are the eigenvalues of A.
   F is defined by

$$F(\lambda_i) = \prod_{\substack{j=1 \\ j \neq i}}^{n} \frac{A - \lambda_j I}{\lambda_i - \lambda_j} \, . \quad (4.3.3)$$

4.3.4 Diagonalisation method
This is applicable only when A has distinct eigenvalues. Let E denote the modal matrix of eigenvalues of A, $E = e_i \quad e_2 \quad ... \quad e_n]$.
   Denote by Λ the diagonal matrix

$$\begin{bmatrix} e^{\lambda_1 t} & 0 \\ 0 & e^{\lambda_n t} \end{bmatrix},$$

then

$$\Phi(t) = E\Lambda E^{-1}. \quad (4.3.5)$$

   More detailed discussion of these methods and description of further methods can be found in Ogata[4].
   A suite of Fortran programs for the calculation of Φ is given in Melsa.[5]

4.4 Solution of linear differential equations — the time varying case

The unforced time varying linear equation is

$$\dot{x}(t) = A(t)x(t), \quad x(t_0) = x_0, \quad (4.4.1)$$

where $x \in R_n$ and A is a square matrix of absolutely integrable functions defined on (t_0, t_1), i.e.,

$$a_{ij}(t) \in L_1(t_0, t_1), \quad \text{for } i, j \leqslant n.$$

Notice that the elements of $A(t)$ are not required to be continuous. In fact if

$$\|A(t)\| < g(t), \quad \forall t,$$

while

$$\int_{t_0}^{t_1} g(t) \, dt < \infty,$$

then eqn. (4.4.1) has a unique solution over (t_0, t_1) that is continuous in t. (See Zadeh and Desoer,[6] page 338.)

The solution of eqn. (4.4.1) can still be written $x(t) = \Phi(t, t_0)x_0$, where Φ is the transition matrix associated with $A(t)$.

However, the transition matrix is more difficult to determine than for the time invariant case and before discussing this aspect we need more theoretical background concerning the transition matrix.

First we define the *fundamental matrix*.

Given an equation

$$\dot{x}(t) = A(t)x(t), \tag{4.4.2}$$

consider the associated equation

$$\dot{X} = A(t)X, \tag{4.4.3}$$

where X is an $n \times n$ matrix.

Given $X(t_0) = X_0$, with $\det X_0 \neq 0$, eqn. (4.4.3) can be solved to yield a solution $X(t)$.

$X(t)$ is called the *fundamental matrix* associated with eqn. (4.4.2). It satisfies the condition,

$$\det X(t) \neq 0, \quad \forall t.$$

Now let $X(t_0) = I$, then the solution $X(t)$ of eqn. (4.4.3) is called the *state transition matrix* of $A(t)$.

Equivalently we can write

$$\frac{\partial}{\partial t}(\Phi(t, t_0)) = A(t)\Phi(t, t_0), \quad \forall t \geqslant t_0, \tag{4.4.4}$$

$$\Phi(t_0, t_0) = I.$$

The state transition matrix transforms the initial condition $x(t_0)$ into the state $x(t)$ and gives the complete solution of the autonomous equation (4.4.1).

To show this, differentiate the solution

$$x(t) = \Phi(t, t_0)x(t_0)$$

yielding

$$\dot{x}(t) = \dot{\Phi}(t, t_0)x(t_0).$$

Using eqn. (4.4.4)

$$\dot{x}(t) = A(t)\Phi(t, t_0)x(t_0) = A(t)x(t),$$

which is the same as eqn. (4.4.1).

As we have seen

$$\dot{\Phi}(t, t_0) = A(t)\Phi(t, t_0), \tag{4.4.5}$$

$$\Phi(t_0, t_0) = I,$$

has the solution $\Phi(t, t_0)$ which is the *transition matrix* we require.

The solution of eqn. (4.4.5) is given by the *Peano–Baker series*.

$$\Phi(t, t_0) = I + \int_{t_0}^{t} A(\tau_1)\, d\tau_1 + \int_{t_0}^{t} A(\tau_1) \int_{t_0}^{t} A(\tau_2)\, d\tau_2\, d\tau_1 + \ldots . \tag{4.4.6}$$

If A is a matrix of constant coefficients then

$$\Phi(t, t_0) = I + A(t - t_0) + \frac{A^2(t - t_0)^2}{2!} + \ldots . \tag{4.4.7}$$

Proof: Since the A are constant we can write

$$\Phi(t, t_0) = I + A \int_{t_0}^{t} d\tau_1 + A^2 \int_{t_0}^{t} \int_{t_0}^{t} d\tau_2\, d\tau_1 + \ldots, \tag{4.4.8}$$

but it is important to note that in general

$$\Phi(t, t_0) = \exp\left[\int_{t_0}^{t} A(\tau)\, d\tau\right], \tag{4.4.9}$$

but the expression does hold if

$$A(t) \int_{t_0}^{t} A(\tau)\, d\tau = \int_{t_0}^{t} A(\tau)\, d\tau\, A(t), \tag{4.4.10}$$

i.e., if the matrices $A(t)$, $\int A(\tau)\, d\tau$ commute.

These matrices commute in case the elements of $A(t)$ are time invariant or if $A(t)$ is a diagonal matrix or in case $A(t)$ can be decomposed into a constant matrix M and a scalar $\alpha(t)$ so that $A(t) = \alpha(t)M$.

It is only in the case where the above matrices commute that $A(t)$ can be brought out of the integral during the derivation to yield

$$\frac{d}{dt}\left(\exp\left[\int_{t_0}^{t} A(\tau)\, d\tau\right]\right) = A(t) \exp\left[\int_{t_0}^{t} A(\tau)\, d\tau\right]. \tag{4.4.11}$$

In the general case the transition matrix is not the exponential of the integral of A.

Therefore, for linear time varying problems, $\Phi(t, t_0)$ has to be determined by numerical evaluation of the expression (4.4.6). Although for simple cases, eqn. (4.4.3) can be expanded and solved analytically.

Not only is this much more time consuming than the evaluation of Φ for time invariant systems, but also the same Φ cannot be used repetitively to advance the solution as in the time invariant case.

If the system is time varying in a known deterministic manner, it may be possible to make a transformation such that the system appears invariant with respect to a new substituted variable. Cases where such transformation can be made are understandably rare.

The section below describes the periodically varying case, where such a transformation can be made with advantage.

4.5 Modelling of linear systems with periodically varying coefficients

In the modelling of rotating devices, such as radar antennae, periodically time-varying parameters are encountered.

Consider a model of the form

$$\dot{x}(t) = A(t)x(t), \quad A(t + T) = A(t), \tag{4.5.1}$$

where T is the period of variation.

The transition matrix $\Phi(t, t_0)$ is periodic in t.

Define a matrix R by the relation

$$e^{RT} = \Phi(T, 0). \tag{4.5.2}$$

Such an R exists if $\Phi(T, 0)$ is non-singular since Φ can then be diagonalised to give

$$\begin{bmatrix} \phi_{11} & & \\ & \ddots & \\ & & \phi_{nn} \end{bmatrix} \quad \text{so that } R \text{ could be chosen as} \quad \begin{bmatrix} \ln \phi_{11} & & \\ & \ddots & \\ & & \ln \phi_{nn} \end{bmatrix}$$

Define an operator $P(t)$ by

$$P^{-1}(t) = \Phi(t, 0) \, e^{-Rt}, \tag{4.5.3}$$

$$\Phi(t, t_0) = \Phi(t, 0)\Phi(0, t_0) \tag{4.5.4}$$

$$= P^{-1}(t) \, e^{Rt} \, e^{-Rt_0} \, P(t_0) \tag{4.5.5}$$

$$= P^{-1}(t) \, e^{R(t-t_0)} \, P(t_0). \tag{4.5.6}$$

From eqn. (4.5.1)

$$x(t) = \Phi(t, t_0)x(t_0) \tag{4.5.7}$$

$$= P^{-1}(t) \, e^{R(t-t_0)} \, P(t_0)x(t_0). \tag{4.5.8}$$

Put

$$z(t) = P(t)x(t), \tag{4.5.9}$$

then

$$P^{-1}(t)z(t) = P^{-1}(t)\, e^{R(t-t_0)}\, P(t_0)P^{-1}(t_0)z(t_0), \tag{4.5.10}$$

$$z(t) = e^{R(t-t_0)}\, z(t_0). \tag{4.5.11}$$

This equation has a time invariant transition matrix and is the solution of the transformed version of eqn. (4.5.1),

$$\dot{z}(t) = Rz(t). \tag{4.5.12}$$

This procedure is known as the *Floquet–Lyapunov transformation*. For further background see Reference 7, Chapter 8.

4.6 Solution of non-linear ordinary differential equations

The principle of several numerical methods for differential equation solution is as follows. Let the equation to be solved be

$$\dot{x} = f(x); \qquad x(t_0) \quad \text{given} \tag{4.6.1}$$

which can be written in the approximate form

$$\frac{\Delta x}{\Delta t} \simeq f(x). \tag{4.6.2}$$

Then

$$x(t_0 + \Delta t) = x(t_0) + \Delta t\, f(x(t_0)) \tag{4.6.3}$$

and subject to numerical considerations, this equation could be used to generate a sequence of discrete time approximations to the true continuous solution of eqn. (4.6.1).

The method described above is of interest for the insight it gives rather than as a numerical method, since errors accumulate rapidly unless the time step Δt is prohibitively short.

A more practically useful method is the *Runge–Kutta* method.

There are several variants of the method but the principle is as follows. Let the non-linear differential equation have the form

$$\frac{dx}{du} = f(x, u) \tag{4.6.4}$$

if x is a function of u then $x(u)$ can be expanded in the Taylor series

$$x(u) = x_0 + \frac{dx}{du}(u - u_0) + \frac{1}{2}\frac{d^2x}{du^2}(u - u_0)^2 + \dots \,. \tag{4.6.5}$$

Define $h = u - u_0$, then

$$x(u_0 + h) = x_0 + h \frac{dx}{du} + \frac{h^2}{2} \frac{d^2x}{du^2} + \dots . \tag{4.6.6}$$

Given an initial condition (x_0, u_0), $x(u_0 + h)$ can be calculated and the process can be repeated so that the values of x at discrete intervals of length h in u can be determined.

The Runge–Kutta method uses the following relations to approximate the first four terms of the Taylor series expansion. Let

$$k_1 = hf(x_0, u_0); \quad k_2 = hf\left(x_0 + \frac{k_1}{2}, u_0 + \frac{h}{2}\right);$$

$$k_3 = hf\left(x_0 + \frac{k_2}{2}, u_0 + \frac{h}{2}\right);$$

$$k_4 = hf(x_0 + k_3, u_0 + h). \tag{4.6.7}$$

Then

$$x(u_0 + h) = h_0 + (\tfrac{1}{6}) (k_1 + 2k_2 + 2k_3 + k_4). \tag{4.6.8}$$

This is a fourth order Runge–Kutta method since eqn. (4.6.8) represents the first four terms of a Taylor series expansion. (For a proof see Reference 8.)

There are several other numerical methods rivalling the Runge–Kutta method. Notably, the so called predictor–corrector methods are generally faster than Runge–Kutta methods although they are not self-starting and this introduces complexity.

The speed of the Runge–Kutta method can be increased dramatically by the inclusion of a subroutine to vary the step length so that where the solution changes only slowly, long time steps are taken. Where n first-order equations are being solved simultaneously all that is necessary is to evaluate at every iteration, the quantity $\max_i |\{f_i\}|$ and use this to vary the value of the time step h.

4.7 References

The classical theory of ordinary differential equations is covered by Reference 9. Reference 10 is a valuable paper by Kalman on axiomatic representation of dynamical systems.

1 BRAUN, M.: *Differential Equations and Their Applications*, Springer, Berlin, 1975.
2 DRIVER, R. D.: *Ordinary and Delay Differential Equations*, Springer, Berlin, 1977.
3 LEIGH, J. R.: *Functional Analysis and Linear Control Theory*, Academic Press, New York, 1980.
4 OGATA, K.: *State Space analysis of Control Systems*, Prentice-Hall, New York, 1967.
5 MELSA, J. L.: *Computer Programs for Computational Assistance in the Study of Linear Control Theory*, McGraw-Hill, New York, 1975.

6 ZADEH, L. A. and DESOER, C. A.: *Linear System Theory*, McGraw-Hill, New York, 1963.

7 BROCKETT, R. W.: *Finite Dimensional Linear Systems*, John Wiley, New York, 1970.

8 RALSTON: *A First Course in Numerical Analysis*, McGraw-Hill, New York, 1963.

9 CODDINGTON, E. A. and LEVINSON, N.: *Theory of Ordinary Differential Equations*, McGraw-Hill, New York, 1955.

10 KALMAN, R. E.: 'Mathematical description of dynamical systems'. *Siam J. Control*, 1963, **1**, No. 2, pp. 152–192.

Chapter 5

Parameter estimation (1): Determination of a single unknown parameter

5.0 Introduction

Parameter estimation is concerned with the problem: Given a plant model where

$$y = f(x, u, a) \qquad (x \text{ is a state vector})$$
$$(u \text{ is an input vector})$$
$$(a \text{ is a parameter vector})$$

(and where it is assumed that the form and structure of the model is correct) determine the best numerical values for the components of the vector a.

For linear steady state models, large numbers of unknown parameters can be determined easily using regression packages. Usually however the problem will be to determine a relatively small number of parameters in a complex nonlinear dynamic model.

Realistic problems will nearly always involve multiple parameters that need to be estimated. However, this chapter deals with the estimation of a single parameter because this is considered to be the best lead-in to the multi-parameter estimation problem.

A parameter estimation problem can always be considered as a maximisation or minimisation problem. We seek to minimise a function of the type

$$J = \int_0^T (\hat{y} - y)^2 \, dt = \int_0^T [\hat{y}(t) - f(x(t), u(t), a)]^2 \, dt.$$

The interval $[0, T]$ is a suitable experiment time to obtain closest possible agreement between the observed output $\hat{y}$ of a process and the output y of a model. Let a be the single parameter to be chosen. Then since y is a function of a, J is also a function of a and can be written $J(a)$ to indicate this. For very simple cases, the methods of calculus can of course be used. Assume that a^* is the value of a that minimises J, i.e. $J(a^*) < J(a)$, $\forall a \neq a^*$, then by Taylor expansion, assuming that J is an analytic function,

$$J(a^* + h) = J(a^*) + hJ'(a^*) + \frac{h^2}{2}J''(a^*) + ..., \qquad (5.0.2)$$

where J' and J'' indicate dJ/da and d^2J/da^2 respectively.

For h very small we have, regardless of the sign of h,

$$J(a^* + h) - J(a^*) = hJ'(a^*) > 0, \qquad (5.0.3)$$

which implies that $J'(a^*) = 0$ so this is a necessary condition for J to be a minimum.

With $J'(a^*) = 0$ the term in h^2 must be considered. It can be seen that if

$$0 < J(a^* + h) - J(a^*) = h^2J''(a^*)/2 + ...,$$

then $J''(a^*)$ must be positive and this is a second condition that must be satisfied in order for $J(a^*)$ to take on a maximum value.

Before leaving analytic results we quote the Weierstrass theorem which is sometimes useful in considering fundamental aspects of function minimisation.

The *Weierstrass theorem* states that every function, continuous on a closed domain, attains its maximum and minimum values on that domain. It is important to note that the usual methods of calculus will only discover the minimum if it lies in the interior of the closed domain.

5.1 Numerical methods

First we assume that the function is *unimodal*, satisfying $J(a^*) < J(a)$, $\forall a \neq a^*$. If this is not the case, multiple minima are present and we must return to the physical situation that we are modelling to understand the significance of this.

Next we consider the *continuity properties* of the function $J(a)$. Are there discontinuities or is the function smooth and well behaved? Often J will be defined only implicitly and we shall not be able to be sure about its behaviour.

Finally we consider the set of admissible values of the argument a. Can a take on all real values or are certain values, e.g. a negative, inadmissible. In case certain regions are inadmissible, we have a *constrained problem* and the boundaries of the inadmissible regions are called the problem constraints.

5.1.1 Methods of numerical search

5.1.1.1 *Direct search*: Given an initial starting point a_0 we can evaluate $J(a_0)$. Let h be a positive increment, put $a_1 = a_0 + h$ and evaluate $J(a_1)$. If $J(a_1) < J(a_0)$ then $a^* > a_0$ because of the unimodality of J.

By comparing the current value $J(a_k)$ of the objective function with the lowest previous value, the *direction* of search can be controlled towards the value *a*.

The *magnitude* of *h* can be large initially, reducing when oscillation about the optimum is detected. Similarly, if progress is very slow, the value of *h* can be increased automatically.

The *criterion for stopping* the search can be when further changes to the argument *a* can produce no significant reduction in *J*, compared with the best value so far obtained.

In any search algorithm, including the simple one outlined above, two problems that must be considered are the *scaling problem* and the *acceleration problem*. Respectively, these are the problems of choosing the initial magnitude of *h* and that of increasing/decreasing the magnitude of *h* as the solution progresses.

In the method outlined above the two problems interact and should too great an initial value of *h* be chosen, the facility for detecting oscillation will compensate for this. The method will in fact scale itself at the cost of additional iterations.

5.1.1.2 Gradient methods: If the function $J(a)$ is differentiable everywhere, then a numerical approximation to the derivative dJ/da at a_0 can be made using the expression

$$\frac{dJ}{da}\bigg|_{a=a_0} = \frac{J(a_0) - J(a_0 + \delta)}{\delta},$$

for a small perturbation δ in *a*.

Given the value of $dJ/da|_{a=a_0}$ we know the direction in which to take the next step. It remains to decide the magnitude of the step and this can be achieved just as for the direct search method described above.

5.1.1.3 Curve fitting: Assume that we have determined three values of *J*, say $J(a_0)$, $J(a_1)$, $J(a_2)$ and assume that the function *J* can be represented by a second-order curve. Let the second-order curve have the form.

$$J(a) = c_0 + c_1(a - a_0) + c_2(a - a_0)(a - a_1). \tag{5.1.2}$$

From the three above known *J* values, the three coefficients $c_1, ..., c_3$ can be determined.

a^* that yields the minimum value for *J* is then found analytically to be

$$a^* = (1/2)(a_0 + a_1 - c_1/c_2). \tag{5.1.3}$$

This procedure can be useful for obtaining a good estimate of the values of *a*, given three values known to be near to a^*.

5.1.1.4 Fibonacci search: A *Fibonacci series* has the form

$$F_r = F_{r-1} + F_{r-2}. \tag{5.1.4}$$

Put $F_0 = 1$ and the relation generates a sequence of Fibonacci numbers.

The Fibonacci search method ranges over a specified interval of length L_1 in the argument a, and makes N function evaluations where N must be specified in advance.

Denote the end points of interval L_1 by c_1, d_1 and define

$$l_1 = \frac{F_{N-2}}{F_N} L_1.$$

Two function evaluations are carried out at

$$a_1 = c_1 + l_1, \qquad b_1 = d_1 - l_1.$$

By unimodality, the interval where a^* is located can be reduced to a length

$$L_2 = L_1 - l_1 = d_1 - a_1 \quad \text{or} \quad b_1 - c_1 = L_1 \frac{F_{N-1}}{F_N}.$$

Denote the end points of this inteval by c_2, d_2. Now

$$l_2 = \frac{F_{N-3}}{F_{N-1}} L_2$$

and

$$a_2 = c_2 + l_2, \qquad b_2 = d_2 - l_2,$$

where a_2, b_2 are the new values of the argument at which J is to be evaluated. This procedure is continued until the N function evaluations have been made.

It can be shown by comparison with alternative methods that the Fibonacci search is extremely efficient in terms of numbers of function evaluations necessary to achieve a particular accuracy. The method achieves this efficiency by, in a sense, using half of the function evaluations twice. This can be demonstrated as follows. The first two function evaluations take place at a_1, b_1. Suppose $J(a_1) > J(b_1)$ then the next interval to be searched is

$$(a_1, d_1) = L_2 = (c_2, d_2).$$

Two new function evaluations are required at a_2, b_2 but

$$a_2 = c_2 + l_2 = \left(c_1 + \frac{F_{N-2}}{F_N} L_1 \right) + \frac{F_{N-3}}{F_{N-1}} \left(\frac{F_{N-1}}{F_N} L_1 \right) \tag{5.1.5}$$

$$= c_1 + \frac{F_{N-1}}{F_N} L_1 = b_1 \tag{5.1.6}$$

Thus, one of the two new function evaluations has already been made in the last cycle—and this is the source of the efficiency of the Fibonacci search.

5.2 References

Since this chapter is introductory to Chapters 6 and 7 detailed references are not given. Chapter 5 of the book below is an adequate supporting reference.

1 BEVERIDGE, G. S. G. and SCHECHTER R. S.: *Optimisation — Theory and Practice*, McGraw-Hill, New York, 1970.

Chapter 6

Parameter estimation (2): Determination of a set of unknown parameters

6.0 Introduction

In practical applications of mathematical modelling, a set of unknown parameters has to be estimated. Although the methods given earlier for estimating a single unknown parameter can to some extent be generalised to many unknowns, the problem is more difficult and new problems arise.

Even where the number of unknown parameters is only two, there are an infinite number of possible search directions instead of only two for the single parameter case.

The unimodality of the objective function cannot be used to eliminate sections of the plane, as the Fibonacci search sequence was able to do for the single parameter case. For this reason, the very efficient Fibonacci method cannot be generalised to deal with the multi-parameter case.

Usually the objective function J is an (unknown) function of parameters a_1, ..., a_n representing different types of physical effects. There is no obvious way of *a priori* scaling the parameters to obtain approximately circular contours of the J function. In the general case then, there are valleys in the contour representation of the J function and this leads to difficulties as will be illustrated shortly.

6.1 Basic principle of sequential search for unknown parameters

Denote by a the vector of parameters $\begin{pmatrix} a_1 \\ ... \\ a_n \end{pmatrix}$, $a \in P = E_n$ where P is called the *parameter space*. Define a scalar function $J(a_1 \, ... \, a_n)$. We seek the parameter vector a that minimises J.

(1)   Select an initial point $a^0 \in E_n$.

(2)   Evaluate $J(a^0)$ numerically.

(3)   Put $J(a^0) = J_{opt}$.

(4)   Choose a vector $e \in E_n$ satisfying $\|e\| = 1$.
                e represents the *direction* of the next search.

(5)   Choose a real number h, $h > 0$.
                h represents the *magnitude* of the next search step.

(6)   Put $a^1 = a^0 + he$.

(7)   Evaluate $J(a^1)$ numerically.

(8)   Compare $J(a^1)$ with J_{opt}

If $J(a^1) < J_{opt}$	If $J(a^1) \geq J_{opt}$
put $J_{opt} = J(a^1)$	put $a^1 = a^0$
adjust e, h	adjust e, h

    This procedure is continued until J_{opt} cannot be significantly decreased by further iteration.

    Considering the above sequence of moves it can be seen that steps (4) and (5) require the choice of search direction and search step size respectively.

    Many different approaches to steps (4) and (5) are possible and here lies the reason for the many different parameter estimation algorithms described in the literature, each having its own particular advantages.

    One obvious point which is, however, often neglected is the following. Where J is very time consuming to evaluate, a search method should be used that extracts the maximum information from every evaluated point. Conversely, where J is very rapidly evaluated, it may be most efficient to search the parameter space using a very crude search technique with many function evaluations. In most modelling applications it will be time consuming to evaluate J, so the methods described here are those where significant use is made of each function evaluation.

6.2 First attempts at multi-parameter search. One-variable-at-a-time search parallel to the axes in parameter space

Let $a = \begin{pmatrix} a_1 \\ a_2 \end{pmatrix}$. Choose a^0 and choose the first search direction as $e_1 = \begin{pmatrix} 1 \\ 0 \end{pmatrix}$. Use any of the one-parameter search methods to find J_{opt} in the direction e, from a^0 parallel to the a_1 axis. Now set $e_2 = \begin{pmatrix} 0 \\ 1 \end{pmatrix}$ and search in this direction again for J_{opt}. This procedure can be continued alternatively in the search directions e_1, e_2.

    The method is illustrated on a well-behaved problem with circular contours (Fig. 6.1).

    However, when the objective function has narrow valleys the method is very inefficient, as shown in Fig. 6.2, where progress is inordinately slow in the two search directions parallel to the co-ordinate axes.

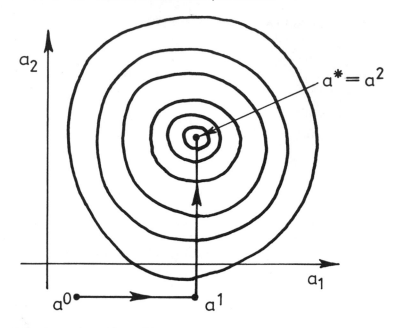

Figure 6.1   *A search problem with circular contours*

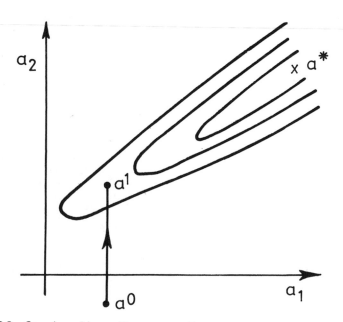

Fig. 6.2   *Search problem with narrow valley*

All practical multi-parameter search methods need to have a facility that prevents the solution becoming virtually stranded in this way.

A selection of particular methods is now described.

6.3 Simplex methods

A simplex is a geometrical figure that in E_2 is an equilateral triangle, in E_3 is a regular tetrahedron with 4 equi-distant vertices, and in E_n is a regular figure with $n + 1$ equidistant vertices.

The principles of simplex methods is illustrated with reference to the two-dimensional parameter search problems.

Choose a^0, a^1, a^2 as the vertices of the two-dimensional simplex and evaluate $J(a^0)$, $J(a^1)$, $J(a^2)$. Compare these and select the largest value. Suppose the largest value is $J(a^0)$. The point a^0 is to be rejected and replaced by its reflection in the opposite side of the simplex to yield a^3. $J(a^3)$ is evaluated and compared with $J(a^1)$, $J(a^2)$. The point corresponding to the greatest value of J is again rejected and by reflection a new point a^4 is produced. The simplex moves through the plane until when near to a^* it oscillates. This condition is used as the criterion for reducing the size of the simplex to allow convergence to a^*.

It is a simple exercise in co-ordinate geometry to program the simplex method and the method is quick in operation because of its simplicity.

There are several variants of the basic simplex method. One well known variant being that due to Nelder and Mead.[1]

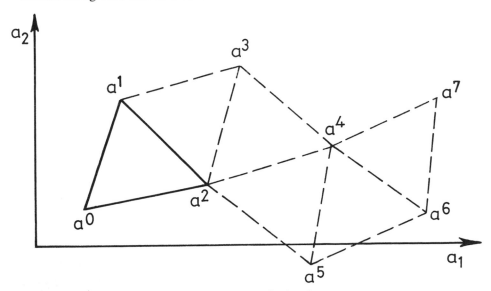

Figure 6.3 *Illustrating how the simplex moves in the plane*

6.4 Hooke and Jeeves method (The method is illustrated with reference to a two-dimensional search)

Assume the initial parameter vector is $b^0 \in E_2$. This is called the *initial base point.*
    Let δ be a small fixed scalar, $\delta > 0$.

Stage 1   Local exploration
Evaluate $J(b^0)$, $J\left(b^0 \pm \delta\binom{1}{0}\right)$, choose the smallest of these three values and denote the argument of the smallest value by c^0. Next evaluate $J\left(c^0 \pm \delta\binom{0}{1}\right)$ and choose the smallest of the three values $J(c^0)$, $J\left(c^0 \pm \delta\binom{0}{1}\right)$. Denote the argument of this smallest value by b^1. This is called the current *base point.*

Stage 2   Major step
Choose $a^1 = b^0 + 2(b^1 - b^0)$.

Stage 3
Evaluate $J(a^1)$.
    If $J(a^1) < J(b^1)$, carry out local exploration about a^1 and establish the new current base point b^2 by repeating the procedure of stage 1.
    If $J(a^1) > J(b^1)$, carry out local exploration about b^1 and establish b^2 in the vicinity of b^1.
    Each major step takes the form
$$a^n = b^{n-1} + 2(b^n - b^{n-1}),$$
and the solution accelerates rapidly if improvement occurs.
    The method is illustrated below for a two-dimensional problem.
    Figure 6.4 shows the rapid acceleration for a problem where the major moves prove successful.
    Figure 6.5 shows the behaviour of the search method when the direction of search needs to follow a curve.
    If at any time, including right at the start, no improvement in J can be found in any of the local search directions, the size of δ is reduced. Eventually, near to a^*, the size of δ should tend to zero and allow the procedure to converge.

6.5 Conjugate directions — general principles

Let the objective function J to be minimised take on its minimum value at $a = a^*$, where a is a vector of parameters.

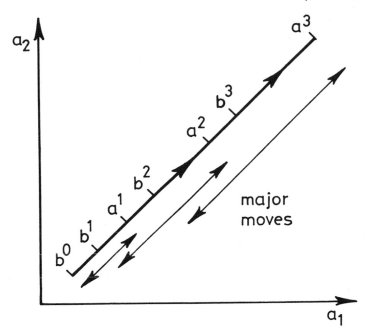

Fig. 6.4 *Hooke and Jeeves method — rapid acceleration*

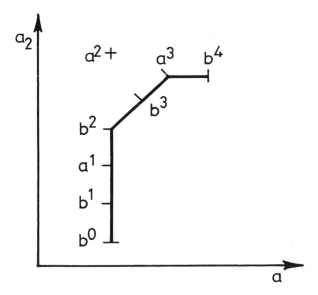

Fig. 6.5 *Hooke and Jeeves method — the search method follows a curved path*

Let $J(a)$ be expressible near to a^* in the form

$$J(a) = J(a^*) + 1/2(a - a^*)^T H(a - a^*) \tag{6.5.1}$$

where H is the Hessian Matrix of second partial derivatives $\partial^2 J/\partial a_i \partial a_j$. Let these coefficients be denoted $c_{i,j}$.

A set of n-dimensional vectors $\{e^i\}$ with components e_i is defined to be *a set of conjugate directions* if given an $n \times n$ matrix C of coefficients c_{ij}

$$(e^i)^T C e^j = 0, \quad \text{all } i,j \leq n, \quad i \neq j \tag{6.5.2}$$

Assume that sequential one-dimensional searches are carried out in the directions $e^1, e^2, \ldots, e^k$. Denote the restricted minimum along each direction by a^k.

Then for some scalar h^k

$$a^k = a^{k-1} + h^k e^k \tag{6.5.3}$$

While at the point a^k

$$\frac{dJ}{dh^k} = \sum_{i=1}^{n} \frac{\partial J}{\partial a_i} \frac{da_i}{dh^k} = \sum_{i=1}^{n} \frac{\partial J}{\partial a_i} e_i^k = 0 \tag{6.5.4}$$

i.e., $< \text{grad } J, e^k > = 0$.

At the minimum value, grad J is orthogonal to the search direction e^k. It can be shown that, after n stages of search

$$\sum_{i}^{n} \frac{\partial J}{\partial a_i} \bigg|_{a=a^n} e_i^j = \sum_{i=1}^{n} \frac{\partial J}{\partial a_i} \bigg|_{a=a^{j+1}} e_i^j + \sum_{l=j+1}^{n-1} \sum_{r=1}^{n} \sum_{i=1}^{n} c_{i,r} h^l e_r^l e_i^j. \tag{6.5.5}$$

If the n stages of search have been in the appropriate conjugate directions then both terms on the right side of eqn. (6.5.5) are zero.

Provided that the $\{e^k\}$ form a linearly independent set, then eqn. (6.5.5) implies that grad $J = 0$ and this is a necessary condition for a minimum of $J(a)$. A sufficient condition can be obtained by imposing a condition that the Hessian of J be positive definite. However in applications the form of J and hence of H is usually unknown.

We note that a search in successive conjugate directions will locate the minimum of a quadratic function of n parameters in exactly n stages. All analytic functions behave approximately like quadratic functions near to a^* so the methods based on this approach have wider application than might have been assumed.

It remains to be decided in the absence of knowledge of the form of the objective function J how to generate a suitable set of conjugate search directions.

We have seen above that the direction e^k joins the minima $J(a^{k-1})$, $J(a^k)$.

Powell's Method[2] implicitly exploits the property of conjugate search directions for quadratic functions near to their minimum value but includes important factors to take account of non-quadratic behaviour likely to be encountered well away from a^*.

Let a^0 be the initial point in n-dimensional parameter space. Let $e_1, \ldots, e_n$ be n given linearly independent search directions.

The method requires successive one dimensional searches to be carried out. From a^0 a search is carried out in direction e_1 to establish a_1^0. From a_1^0 a search is carried out in direction e_2 to establish a_2^0. This procedure is completed in each of the n search directions. The value a_n^0 is denoted a^1 and a vector μ is determined from

$$\mu = a^1 - a^0. \tag{6.5.6}$$

μ will form a new search direction provided that certain inequalities, given below, are satisfied. Δ and m are determined from the equation.

$$\Delta = \max_i \{J(a_i^0) - J(a_{i-1}^0)\}, \tag{6.5.7}$$

with m denoting the value of i that maximises the right-hand side. Define

$$J_t = J(2a^1 - a^0). \tag{6.5.8}$$

The first inequality (6.5.9) tests whether the tentative value J_t of the objective function produces an improvement.

$$J_t \leqslant J(a^0). \tag{6.5.9}$$

If this inequality is not satisfied the new search direction μ will not be used.

The second inequality (6.5.10) is designed to suppress the direction μ if there is an indication that μ is pointing across a steep valley.

$$(J(a^0) - 2J(a^1) + J_t)(J(a^0) - J(a^1) - \Delta)^2 \geqslant \frac{\Delta}{2} (J(a^0) - J_t)^2. \tag{6.5.10}$$

If this inequality is satisfied then the new search direction μ will not be used.

Thus there are two possibilities.

(a) *New direction μ not to be used.* In this case the procedure is repeated starting from the base point a^1, using the search directions $e_1, \ldots, e_n$ to establish a point a^2 and to generate new values of Δ, m, μ.

(b) *Direction μ to be incorporated.* The procedure is repeated, starting from the base point a^1, using the search directions

$$e_1, \ldots, e_{m-1}, e_{m+1}, \ldots, e_{n-1}, \mu.$$

The procedure is repeated with a new vector μ being produced at each iteration. The set $\{\mu\}$ of such vectors forms a set of conjugate directions.

6.6 The Rosenbrock rotating axis method[3]

This is a well tried method that works well on a wide variety of objective functions including those exhibiting narrow curving valleys. In a search for n unknown parameters, n directional vectors v_i, $i =, ..., n$ are stored, satisfying $\|v_i\| = 1$ and n scalar step lengths e_i, $i = 1, ..., n$.

6.6.1 Initial phase
Initially the vectors v_i are chosen to coincide with the axes in parameter space while the initial step lengths e_i are allocated a small arbitrary value.

An initial base point a^0 is chosen and then the search commences in one variable at a time over the n directions v_i with step lengths e_i.

Each time the objective function $J(a^k)$ is less than the best previous $J(a)$, $J(a^k)$ becomes the new base point from which perturbations are made. Each time a step e_i results in improvement in J, the e_i that produced the improvement is multiplied by 3. Conversely each time a step e_i results in worsening of J, the e_i that produced the failure is multiplied by -0.5.

In this way, acceleration is accomplished in favourable directions and deceleration and reversal when unfavourable results are encountered. Notice that all this occurs while still using one variable at a time search with the original axes. This procedure continues until failure preceded by success is encountered in every search direction, when the procedure is assumed to be stranded in a valley (although the alternative explanation is that it has converged to the required solution a^*).

At this point, phase 2 begins.

6.6.2 Phase 2 — Rotation of axes to allow following of valleys
When the axes are to be rotated, a new set of orthonormal vectors is generated. One of these vectors is aligned with any local valley in the function. The vectors form a new set of search directions in parameter space.

The orthonormal set of new axes is generated as follows.

Let the new axes be denoted $v_1^2, ..., v_p^2$ and the old axes $v_1^1, ..., v_p^1$. Define $d_1, ..., d_p$ by $d_i = \Sigma_{j=1}^{r} (e_i)_j$, where the summation in j runs over the number of steps r since the axes were last rotated. Let

$$\alpha_1 = d_1 v_1^1 + d_2 v_2^1 + ... + d_p v_p^1$$

$$\alpha_2 = \phantom{d_1 v_1^1 + {}} d_2 v_2^1 + ... + d_p v_p^1$$

$$\overline{}$$

$$\alpha_p = d_p v_p^1$$

Define

$$\beta_1 = \alpha_1, \quad v_1^2 = \beta_1/\|\beta_1\|,$$

$$\beta_2 = \alpha_2 - \langle \alpha_2, v_1^2 \rangle v_1^2, \quad v_2^2 = \beta_2/\|\beta_2\|,$$

$$\beta_p = \alpha_p - \sum_{i=1}^{p-1} \langle \alpha_p, v_i^2 \rangle v_i^2,$$

$$v_p^2 = \beta_p / \|\beta_p\|,$$

where

$$\|\beta\| = \left(\sum_{i=1}^{p} \beta_i^2 \right)^{1/2} = \langle \beta, \beta \rangle^{1/2}, \quad \langle \alpha, v \rangle = \sum_{i=1}^{p} \alpha_i v_i$$

Thus the new axis v_1^2 tends to align itself along any valley in the objective function while the remaining axes are generated by a Gram–Schmidt method to complete an orthonormal set spanning the parameter space. Axis rotation is again initiated when the search has failed in each direction.

New axes will be generated frequently where the solution is required to follow a curved valley of the objective function.

6.7 Steepest descent method[4]

None of the methods described so far assumed the availability of derivatives of the objective function. We can expect that if derivatives are available, they can be used to assist the direction of search.

Given an objective function $J(a)$; a, n-dimensional, and an initial base point a^0, the method of steepest descent moves the solution in the direction that produces the maximum rate of change.

We require to evaluate, either analytically or by small perturbation of one variable at a time, the gradient

$$\nabla_a J(a) = \begin{pmatrix} \partial J/\partial a_1 \\ \vdots \\ \partial J/\partial a_n \end{pmatrix}$$

$\nabla_a J(a)$ gives the direction of steepest descent. The next question to be settled is how far to move in that direction. In the method of steepest descent, a full one-dimensional search is carried out until the minimum value of J is found and then the process is repeated. A little thought shows that successive search directions will be orthogonal, since each direction of search reaches its optimum parallel to a contour, while each direction of steepest descent starts perpendicular to a contour. In fact, this method is prone to excessive zig-zag behaviour as illustrated in Fig. 6.6.

6.8 Another gradient method

A method very similar to that just described is where, having found the initial direction of steepest descent, a fixed step length h is chosen and a move made to $a^1 = a^0 - h\nabla_a J(a)|_{a=a^0}$. At the point a^1 the direction of steepest descent is again evaluated and another small step made in that direction. This method is more truly a method of steepest descent than the method that bears that name, since the solution tends to cross each contour at right angles.

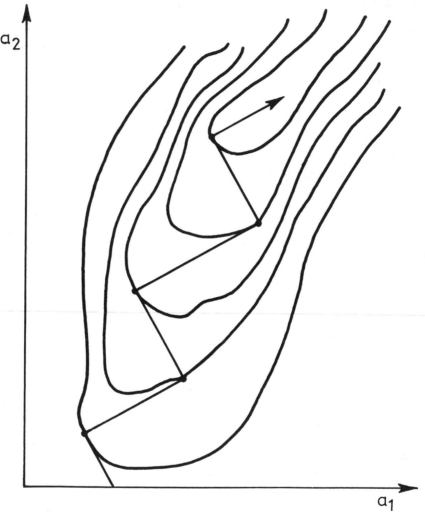

Fig. 6.6 *Steepest descent method moving along a valley*

Again this method does not perform so well in practice as might be expected. An example is given below of the method in operation first on a circular function, where of course it works well, and then on a simple function with broad elliptical contours. The reader is invited to try different values of increment h — none will produce a satisfactory solution for the elliptical case.

6.8.1 Gradient method — family of circles centred at x_1^*, x_2^*

Let $x_1^* = 2$, $x_2^* = 3$, the equation is

$$(x_1 - x_1^*)^2 + (x_2 - x_2^*)^2 = J,$$

$$x_1^2 - 4x_1 + 4 + x_2^2 - 6x_2 + 9 = J,$$

$$x_1^2 - 4x_1 + x_2^2 - 6x_2 + 13 = J,$$

$\nabla_x J = 2x_1 - 4$, choose $a^0 = \begin{pmatrix} 0 \\ 0 \end{pmatrix}$ as the starting point, $2x_2 - 6$,

$$a^1 = a^0 - h \left. \nabla_x J \right|_{a=a^0} = \begin{pmatrix} 0 \\ 0 \end{pmatrix} - h \begin{pmatrix} -4 \\ -6 \end{pmatrix}.$$

If $h = 0.5$ then $a^1 = \begin{pmatrix} 2 \\ 3 \end{pmatrix}$.

This very rapid arrival at the correct solution is to be expected since all normals to a set of concentric circles pass through the centre.

6.8.2 Gradient method — family of ellipses centred at x_1^*, x_2^*

x_1^*, x_2^* as before but put $\alpha = 4$ in

$$\alpha(x_1 - x_1^*)^2 + (x_2 - x_2^*)^2 = J$$

to yield

$$4x_1^2 - 16x_1 + x_2^2 - 6x_2 + 25 = J,$$

$$\nabla_x J = \begin{pmatrix} 8x_1 - 16 \\ 2x_2 - 6 \end{pmatrix}, \quad a^0 = \begin{pmatrix} 0 \\ 0 \end{pmatrix} \text{ as before.}$$

With $h = 0.2$ we obtain the sequence of points given in the table. This sequence is shown in Fig. 6.7.

It can be seen that the solution oscillates in the x_1 direction but approaches the correct value exponentially in the x_2 direction. The step length h must be chosen as a compromise between two conflicting requirements (in an n-dimensional search, between n conflicting requirements).

Even in the obviously straightforward case of an ellipse, not violently non-circular, with axes parallel to the co-ordinate axes in parameter space, the gradient method proves to be inefficient.

6.9 Gradient methods — general comments

A number of sophisticated gradient algorithms exist. For further details consult the table of references and the associated tree diagram. Notable among these methods are those using conjugate gradients. The method of Fletcher and Reeves[5] starts by making a uni-directional search in the direction of steepest descent. The second and subsequent directions of search are

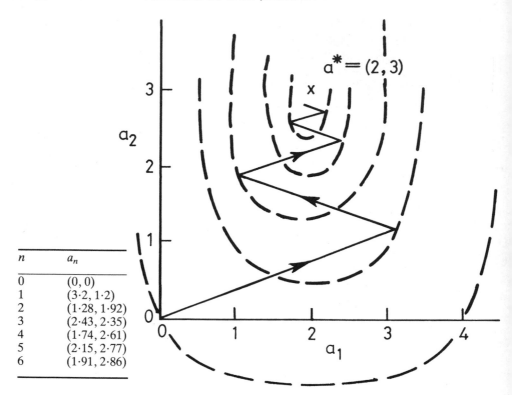

n	a_n
0	$(0, 0)$
1	$(3 \cdot 2, 1 \cdot 2)$
2	$(1 \cdot 28, 1 \cdot 92)$
3	$(2 \cdot 43, 2 \cdot 35)$
4	$(1 \cdot 74, 2 \cdot 61)$
5	$(2 \cdot 15, 2 \cdot 77)$
6	$(1 \cdot 91, 2 \cdot 86)$

Fig. 6.7 *Progress of the gradient method on an elliptical objective function*

determined so as to form a conjugate set, the calculation requiring a knowledge only of the gradients of the objective function. Another conjugate gradient method is due to Fletcher and Powell.[6]

In general, gradient methods are to be preferred whenever derivatives can be evaluated analytically. Where derivatives have to be determined by numerical perturbation, the extra time taken to obtain the derivatives and the errors due to local noise will usually make the methods unattractive.

6.10 Parameter estimation in the presence of constraints

If in a multi-parameter search the domain of the variable a is restricted, for instance we might have the restriction for each element a_i

$$b_i \leqslant a_i \leqslant c_i$$

where b_i, c_i are given constants then the problem is called a *constrained parameter estimation problem*.

Constrained problems are considerably more difficult than unconstrained problems. The basic difficulty is how to prevent the solution moving into inadmissible regions in parameter space while allowing it to operate efficiently right up to the boundary of the remaining region.

Constrained methods find most application in optimisation whereas in modelling, parameters can usually be allowed free movement. If impossible values of model parameters result from a search (e.g., negative mass), this should usually be taken as a sign of errors in the form of the model and not as the signal to include constraints on the domain of the parameters.

The Rosenbrock program has a comprehensive facility to include inequality constraints and is generally recommended for those occasions when constraints do need to be imposed on a multi-parameter search.

6.11 Multi-parameter search — discussion

With so many differing methods available it is not surprising that several authors have carried out critical comparisons of the available methods. However, there is no universally acceptable measure of performance and everything depends on the problem under consideration. The 'tree' given in Fig. 6.8 is based on a more comprehensive tree contained in Reference 7.

6.12 References

1 NELDER, J. A. and MEAD, R.: 'A simple method for function minimisation', *The Computer Journal*, 1965, **7**, pp. 308–313.
2 POWELL, M. J. D.: 'An efficient method of finding the minimum of a function of several variables without calculating derivatives', *The Computer Journal*, 1964, **7**, pp. 303–307.
3 ROSENBROCK, H. H.: 'An automatic method for finding the greatest and the least value of a function', *The Computer Journal*, 1960, **3**, pp. 175–184.
4 ROSENBROCK, H. H. and STOREY, C.: *Computational Techniques for Chemical Engineers*, Pergamon Press, New York, 1966.
5 FLETCHER, R. and REEVES, C. M.: 'Function minimisation by conjugate gradients', *The Computer Journal*, 1964, **7**, pp. 149–154.
6 FLETCHER, R. and POWER, M. J. D.: 'A rapidly convergent descent method for minimisation', *Computer Journal*, 1963, **6**, pp. 163–168.
7 GHANI, S. N. and BARNES, L.: 'Parameter optimisation for unconstrained object functions — a bibliography', *Computer Aided Design*, 1972, **4**, No. 5, pp. 247–260.
8 WEISS, E. A., ARCHER, D. H. and BURT, D. A.: *Petr. Refiner*, 1961, **40**, No. 10, pp. 169–174.
9 DAVIDON, W. C.: 'Variable metric method for minimisation', *Res. and Dev. Rep. ANL-5990*, A.E.C., 1969.
10 ZANGWILL, W. I.: 'Minimising a function without calculating derivatives', *The Computer Journal*, 1967, **10**, pp. 293–296.
11 SWANN, W. H.: 'Report on the development of a new direct search method of optimisation', *Central Instrument Laboratory Research Note*, 64/3, ICI Ltd., 1964.

12 SHAH, B. V., BUEHLER, R. K. and KEMPTHORNE, O.: 'Some algorithms for minimising a function of several variables', *J. Soc. Ind. Appl. Math.*, 1964, **12**, pp. 74–92.
13 KREYSZIG, E: *Advanced Engineering Mathematics*, John Wiley, New York, 1979.
14 BROYDEN, C. G.: 'Quasi–Newton methods and their application to function minimisation', *Math. Comp.*, 1967, **21**, pp. 368–381.

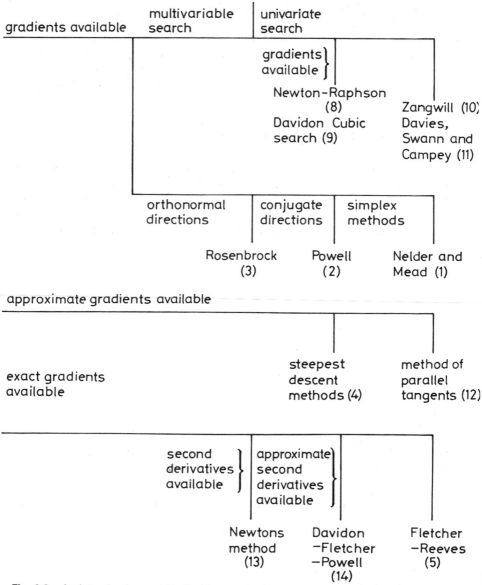

Fig. 6.8 *An introduction to hill-climbing methods*
(Numbers in parenthesis correspond with entries in the list of references)

Chapter 7

Parameter estimation (3): On-line methods

7.0 Introduction

Any method from Chapter 6 can be used in an on-line computer scheme provided that the practical problems associated with program development and running can be overcome. Some methods are particularly suitable for on-line use and two such methods are described below. Both methods apply to systems that can be described by ordinary differential equations. The augmented state method can be used for non-linear systems and the least squares method can be used in the case where the system includes a finite delay.

7.1 Determination of the parameters in the A matrix of a linear system by the *augmented state method*

Let $\dot{x}(t) = Ax$ with the elements of the n-dimensional matrix A to be determined numerically from measurements. Represent each non-zero element of the A matrix as an additional (dummy) state variable. With this modification, there will be product non-linearities, and the equation can be written in the more general form

$$\dot{x}(t) = f(x). \tag{7.1.1}$$

Assume a value for $x(0)$ and linearise about the resultant solution $x_s(t)$. If we define $y(t) = x(t) - x_s(t)$ then

$$\dot{y}_j(t) = \sum_{i=1}^{m} \partial f_j/\partial x_i y_i(t) \tag{7.1.2}$$

or

$$\dot{y}(t) = Gy(t)$$

with solution $y(t) = \Phi(t)y(0)$, where $y(0)$ is a perturbation from the assumed value $x(0)$.

Now, given measurements $\hat{x}(t)$ of system response, construct a cost function

$$J = \int_0^T \gamma(\hat{x}(t) - x(t))^2 \, dt = \int_0^T \gamma(\hat{x}(t) - x_s(t) + y(t))^2 \, dt, \qquad (7.1.3)$$

where γ is a vector of weighting factors. $\gamma_i = 1$ for x_i, an original state variable. $\gamma_i = 0$ for x_i, a dummy state variable.

$$J = \int_0^T \sum_{i=1}^m \gamma(\hat{x}(t) - x_s(t) + \Phi(t)y(0))^2 \, dt$$

$$= \int_0^T \sum_{i=1}^m \gamma_i(\hat{x}_i(t) - x_{s_i}(t) + \sum_{j=1}^m \phi_i y_j(0))^2 \, dt, \qquad (7.1.4)$$

where the ϕ_{ij} are elements in the $\Phi(T)$ matrix, e^{GT}.

Differentiating with respect to each $y_j(0)$ yields

$$\partial J / \partial Y_0 = 2 \int \sum \gamma_i [\hat{x}_i(t) + \sum_{j=1}^m \phi_{ij}(t)y_j(0) - x_{s_i}(t)](\phi_{ij}) \, dt \qquad (7.1.5)$$

and equating these partial derivatives to zero gives m equations in the m unknowns

$$y_j^*(0); j = 1, \ldots, m.$$

(This being a necessary condition for J to be minimised.) When the $y_j^*(0)$ have been determined numerically we argue as follows.

The best estimate $x^*(0)$ of the initial conditions that gave rise to the measured response $x(t)$ is given by $x^*(0) = x(0) + y^*(0)$ since this is how the elements of $y^*(0)$ were chosen.

The dummy state variables, that are in reality constant coefficients in the matrix A, necessarily satisfy $\dot{x}_i(t) = 0$ so that an estimate of the initial state of the augmented system contains estimates of the coefficients in the A matrix of the original system.

Note that the procedure described may need to be iterated to give accurate estimates of the elements in the A matrix. Thus, after calculating

$$x^*(0) = x(0) + y^*(0),$$

the resultant value of $x^*(0)$ will be substituted for $x(0)$ in the solution of eqn. (7.1.1) and the process repeated.

The method is useful in practice for updating a large A matrix in which only a small number of coefficients is unknown. It is therefore more useful in on-line model updating than in the parameter estimation stages of model building.

In an on-line situation the procedure is as follows.

Measure response $\hat{x}(t)$ over interval T seconds.

Calculate $y(0)$. (Each dummy state variable corresponds to a parameter, assumed constant on $(0, T)$. Hence the estimate of the initial state contains an estimate of the system parameters.)

Measure response $\hat{x}(t)$ over next interval of T seconds and continue.

Of course, not all the initial conditions need to be estimated if they are measurable and if the effects of noise can be ignored.

7.2 Generalised least-squares method — an algorithm for on-line identification of the parameters in a linear discrete time model

This section is based on Hastings–James.[1]

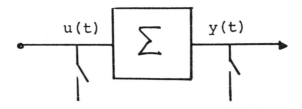

Fig. 7.1   *The sampling of signals from a continuous process*

The continuous time system Σ shown in Fig. 7.1 is to be modelled from sampled input–output data by a discrete time approximation

$$y_t = -a_1 y_{t-1} - a_2 y_{t-2}, \ldots, -a_n y_{t-n}$$
$$+ b_1 u_{t-1} + b_2 u_{t-2}, \ldots, + b_n u_{t-n}. \tag{7.2.0}$$

The model gives the output at any time t as a linear function of past inputs and outputs. The order of the model is chosen by the modeller and the algorithm is required to determine the $2n$ unknown parameters a_i, b_i, $i = 1, \ldots, n$. If $2n$ samples of u and y are available then evidently eqn. (7.2.0) can be solved for the a_i, b_i. Let

$$y = \{y_t, y_{t+1}, \ldots, y_{t+2n-1}\}. \tag{7.2.1}$$

Then as a result of the $2n$ observations, the $2n$ versions of equation (7.2.0) can be combined to yield

$$y = \Lambda\theta, \tag{7.2.2}$$

where

$$\Lambda = [-z^{-1}y \vdots \ldots \vdots -z^{-n}y \vert z^{-1}u \vdots \ldots \vdots -z^{-n}u], \tag{7.2.3}$$

$$\theta^T = [a_1, a_2, \ldots, a_n, b_1, b_2, \ldots, b_n]. \tag{7.2.4}$$

z is the shift operator,

$$u = [u_t, u_{t+1}, \ldots, u_{t+2n-1}].$$

The required parameters θ are obtained by inversion as soon as the Λ matrix has been accumulated

$$\theta = \Lambda^{-1}y. \tag{7.2.5}$$

What has gone above illustrates the principle of the method but eqn. (7.2.5) is not a practically useful algorithm for most purposes since:

> Suppose $u(t)$, $y(t)$ happen to be constant over the whole period of experimentation. There is no information in the data and the matrix Λ is singular. Even when there is variation the matrix Λ is easily ill conditioned.

A solution to this problem is to record many more than $2n$ samples of data. Assume that we have p samples of data where p is very much greater than $2n$. The equation $y = \Lambda\theta$ still applies but Λ now has dimension $p \times 2n$.

The parameter vector θ is now obtained by manipulating eqn. (7.2.2),

$$\Lambda^T y = \Lambda^T \Lambda \theta,$$
$$\theta = [\Lambda^T \Lambda]^{-1} \Lambda^T y. \tag{7.2.6}$$

Equation (7.2.6) can be recognised as a standard result in linear regression analysis and in fact θ, given by eqn. (7.2.6) is the best least-squares estimate of the vector of parameters.

For on-line use, the algorithm (7.2.6) has the disadvantage of requiring a large matrix to be inverted. A recursive version of the algorithm that avoids the inversion, except during initialisation, has been developed.

7.3 Recursive least-squares algorithm

Assume that Λ, y have been obtained and substituted in eqn. (7.2.6) above to yield an estimate θ_0 for the vector of parameters. Given one further scan of the input and output of the system, we wish to develop a recursive equation of the form

$$\theta_1 = f(\theta_0, u_1, y_1), \tag{7.3.1}$$

where u_1, y_1 are the latest scanned values of input and output and θ_1 is the latest estimate of the parameter vector.

Such an equation can be used every time a new data scan is taken to update the vector of parameters. By this means matrix inversion is avoided except during the algorithm start-up.

To obtain an equation of the form (7.3.1), we note that θ_0, θ_1 are given by

$$\theta_0 = [\Lambda^T \Lambda]^{-1} \Lambda^T y,$$

$$\theta_1 = \left(\begin{bmatrix} \Lambda \\ \lambda^T \end{bmatrix}^T \begin{bmatrix} \Lambda \\ \lambda^T \end{bmatrix} \right)^{-1} \begin{pmatrix} \Lambda \\ \lambda^T \end{pmatrix}^T \begin{pmatrix} y \\ y_1 \end{pmatrix}, \tag{7.3.2}$$

where λ is the vector corresponding to the bottom row of the expanded matrix Λ

$$\theta_1 = [\Lambda^T\Lambda + \lambda\lambda^T]^{-1}[\Lambda^T\lambda]\begin{bmatrix} y \\ y_1 \end{bmatrix}. \tag{7.3.3}$$

We now make use of the following identity (see reference 1)

$$[\Lambda^T\Lambda + \lambda\lambda^T]^{-1} = [\Lambda^T\Lambda]^{-1} - \frac{[\Lambda^T\Lambda]^{-1}\lambda\lambda^T[\Lambda^T\Lambda]^{-1}}{1 + \lambda^T[\Lambda^T\Lambda]^{-1}\lambda} \tag{7.3.4}$$

From eqn. (7.3.2) and the identity (7.3.4) we obtain the desired recursive equation for θ_1

$$\theta_1 = \theta_0 + \frac{[\Lambda^T\Lambda]^{-1}\lambda[Y_1 - \lambda^T\theta_0]}{1 + \lambda^T[\Lambda^T\Lambda]^{-1}\lambda} \tag{7.3.5}$$

The matrix Λ is updated using the equation

$$(\Lambda_1^T\Lambda_1)^{-1} = (\Lambda_0^T\Lambda_0)^{-1} - \frac{(\Lambda_0^T\Lambda_0)^{-1}\lambda\lambda^T(\Lambda_0^T\Lambda_0)^{-1}}{1 + \lambda^T(\Lambda_0^T\Lambda_0)^{-1}\lambda} \tag{7.3.6}$$

where Λ_0, Λ_1 are the old and updated matrices respectively.

7.3.1 Extension of the model to take account of finite delay in the process

If the process has a finite delay that can be approximated by an integral number, say k, of sampling intervals then the model is easily modified to take this into account

Equation (7.2.0) becomes

$$\begin{aligned} y_t &= - a_1 y_{t-1}, \ldots, - a_n b_{t-n} \\ &\quad + b_1 u_{t-k-1} + \ldots + b_n u_{t-k-n} \end{aligned} \tag{7.3.7}$$

and the development goes through exactly as before.

7.3.2 Effects of noise on the algorithm

In the above analyses no specific consideration was given to the effects of noise on the estimation.

Assume now that the system to be modelled is corrupted by uncorrelated filtered white noise which appears additively at the output.

The output $v(t)$ with noise is therefore given by

$$v(t) = b(t) + \alpha(t), \tag{7.3.8}$$

where $\alpha(t)$ is the noise term.

Referring to the algorithm (7.2.6), when noise is considered, we have for the estimation of θ the expression

$$\theta = [\Lambda^T\Lambda]^{-1}\Lambda^T y + [\Lambda^T\Lambda]^{-1}\Lambda^T \alpha. \tag{7.3.9}$$

Let the true vector of parameters be $\bar{\theta}$ then the uncorrupted output is given by

$$y = \Lambda \,\bar{\theta}.$$

Hence the estimate θ is given by

$$\theta = [\Lambda^T\Lambda]^{-1} \,\Lambda^T\Lambda \,\bar{\theta} + [\Lambda^T\Lambda]^{-1} \,\Lambda^T \,\alpha,$$

$$\theta = \bar{\theta} + [\Lambda^T\Lambda]^{-1} \,\Lambda^T \,\alpha. \tag{7.3.10}$$

Thus the estimate θ is biased by the expected value of the second term. However, the bias can be removed by estimating the parameters in a noise model and making an appropriate transformation (see Reference 1).

In practice the removal of estimation bias caused by corrupting noise requires that the data be suitably filtered before being input to either the generalised least-squares algorithm or the recursive version.

What is given above should be regarded as a theoretical foundation and initial stance for the construction of a recursive least-squares algorithm.

In particular, the convergence of the algorithm will always need to be studied with care. In this connection, it has been found that the convergence can be improved by using matrices other than Λ in the algorithm. For instance, multiples of the identity matrix have been used successfully instead of Λ.

7.3.3 Use of the recursive algorithm to model a process with slowly changing parameters

In the sections above we have been concerned with the convergence of an estimate θ to the true value of vector of parameters $\bar{\theta}$.

In case $\bar{\theta}$ is varying with time, we want the estimate θ to track $\bar{\theta}$ as well as possible. Under the circumstances it is necessary somehow to weight the data so that the effect of old data is less than the effect of recent data.

This can be achieved by adding an *ad hoc* weighting multiplier in eqn. (7.3.5) so that the effect of the accumulated observation is reduced, compared with the effect of the latest observation. The choice of weighting multiplier is a compromise between speed of response, stability and accuracy.

7.4 References

1 HASTINGS-JAMES, R. and SAGE, M. W.: 'Recursive generalised least-squares procedure for on-line identification of process parameters', *Proc. IEE (Control and Science)*, 1969, **116**, No. 12, pp. 2057–2061.

Chapter 8

Linearisation and linearity in parameters

8.0 Linearisation — general principles

During modelling, nonlinear relations are often replaced by linear approximations in the interests of mathematical tractability of the model. Obviously, nearly linear functions might be replaced by straight line approximations. *Piecewise* linearisation splits the function into a number of linear approximations. As the model operates and moves into different regions, the approximations used have to be changed. Where the nonlinear relations are defined by experimental data, linearisation can be carried out by regression. Where the non linearity is defined analytically, it can be *expanded in a Taylor Series* in which all but the linear terms are neglected.

Let

$$x = f(u) \tag{8.0.1}$$

be a differentiable nonlinear relation between u and x.

Expanding about any chosen point u_0 in a Taylor series gives

$$x = f(u_0) + (u - u_0) \left. \frac{df}{du} \right|_{u_0} + \text{higher order terms.} \tag{8.0.2}$$

Let

$$x_0 = f(u_0) \text{ then}$$

$$x_0 + x - x_0 = f(u_0) + (u - u_0) \left. \frac{df}{du} \right|_{u_0} + \text{higher order terms,} \tag{8.0.3}$$

$$x - x_0 = u - u_0 \left. \frac{df}{du} \right|_{u0} + \dots ,$$

or

$$\delta x = \delta u \left. \frac{df}{du} \right|_{u_0} + \text{higher order terms} + \dots , \tag{8.0.4}$$

where $(\delta u, \delta x)$ is the perturbation from the chosen linearisation point (u_0, x_0).

Where f is a function of several variables, Taylor's series can again be used. Let $x = f(u_1, u_2, \ldots, u_n)$ then Taylor's series expansion gives

$$x = f(u_1^0, \ldots, u_n^0) + (u_1 - u_1^0) \left.\frac{\partial f}{\partial u_1}\right|_{u_1^0} + \ldots, + (u_n^0) \left.\frac{\partial f}{\partial u_n}\right|_{u_n^0}$$

$$+ \text{ higher order terms.} \qquad (8.0.5)$$

To yield the linear approximation

$$\delta x = \delta u_1 \left.\frac{\partial f}{\partial u_1}\right|_{u_1^0} + \ldots + \delta u_n \left.\frac{\partial f}{\partial u_n}\right|_{u_n^0}, \qquad (8.0.6)$$

where $(\delta u_1, \ldots, \delta u_n, \delta x)$ is the perturbation from the point $(u_1^0, \ldots, u_n^0, x^0)$.

In performing linearisation it is always advisable to check the magnitude of the higher order terms to estimate the degree of approximation that is being made.

8.1 Linearisation of a set of nonlinear differential equations

Given a set of non-linear equations

$$\frac{dx_i}{dt} = f_i(x_1, \ldots, x_n, u_1, \ldots, u_r), \quad i = 1, \ldots, n, \qquad (8.1.1)$$

$$y_i = g_i(x_1, \ldots, x_n, u_1, \ldots, u_r), \quad i = 1, \ldots, m, \qquad (8.1.2)$$

where u_i, x_i, y_i, represent input, internal and output variables respectively and f_i, g_i represent non-linear functions.

Denote

$$u = \begin{pmatrix} u_1 \\ \vdots \\ u_r \end{pmatrix}, \quad x = \begin{pmatrix} x_1 \\ \vdots \\ x_n \end{pmatrix}, \quad y = \begin{pmatrix} y_1 \\ \vdots \\ y_m \end{pmatrix}.$$

For a particular initial condition $x_s(0)$ and a particular $u_s(t)$, $t \in (0, T)$, denote the solution of eqns. (8.1.1) and (8.1.2) by

$$x_s(t), \quad y_s(t), \quad t \in (0, T).$$

If the f_i, g_i are differentiable functions then eqns. (8.1.1) and (8.1.2) can be linearised about the particular solution $x_s(t)$, $y_s(t)$ to the standard multivariable form as follows.

For a general initial condition $x(0)$ and a general input $u(t)$ we can write

$$x(0) = x_s(0) + z(0),$$

$$u(t) = u_s(t) + v(t), \qquad (8.1.3)$$

where z, v are perturbations.

Combining the results obtained

$$\frac{d}{dt}(x_s(t) + z(t)) = f(x_s(t) + z(t), u_s(t) + v(t)), \tag{8.1.4}$$

$$y_s(t) + w(t) = g(x_s(t) + z(t) + v(t)), \tag{8.1.5}$$

$$\frac{d}{dt}(x_s(t) + z(t)) = f(x_s(t), u_s(t)) + Az(t) + Bv(t) +$$

$$\text{remainder terms.} \tag{8.1.6}$$

Noting that

$$f(x_s(t), u_s(t)) = \frac{dx_s(t)}{dt} \text{ , eqn. (8.1.6) simplifies to}$$

$$\frac{dz(t)}{dt} = Az(t) + Bv(t) + \text{remainder terms.} \tag{8.1.7}$$

Similarly, since $y_s(t) = g(x_s(t), u_s(t))$ we have that

$$w(t) = Cz(t) + Du(t) + \text{remainder terms.}$$

The A, B, C, D matrices represent the coefficients of the first linear terms of appropriate Taylor series expansions, while the remainder terms are higher order and linearisation automatically neglects them.

Thus as required we have

$$\frac{dz(t)}{dt} = Az(t) + Bv(t),$$

$$w(t) = Cz(t) + Dv(t)$$

with A, B, C, D matrices being determined by partial differentation as follows:

$$a_{ij} = \frac{\partial f_i}{\partial x_j}\bigg|_{x_s(t),u_s(t)},$$

$$b_{ij} = \frac{\partial f_i}{\partial u_j}\bigg|_{x_s(t),u_s(t)}, \tag{8.1.8}$$

$$c_{ij} = \frac{\partial g_i}{\partial x_j}\bigg|_{x_s(t),u_s(t)},$$

$$d_{ij} = \frac{\partial g_i}{\partial u_j}\bigg|_{x_s(t),u_s(t)}.$$

Note that in the linearised version, the original non-linear time invariant equations have been replaced by linear equations with time varying coefficients. The linearised equations have constant coefficients only in the case that the equations are linearised about a constant solution, $x_s(t) = k$.

In case the coefficients $\partial f_i / \partial x_j$, etc., cannot be obtained analytically, it may be possible to approximate them by numerical perturbation of solutions of the non-linear model using relations such as

$$\frac{\partial f_i}{\partial x_j} \simeq$$

$$\frac{f(x_1, \ldots , x_j + \Delta x_j, \ldots , x_n, u_1, \ldots , u_r) - f(x_1, \ldots , x_j, \ldots , x_n, u_1, \ldots , u_r)}{\Delta x_j}$$

$$(8.1.9)$$

It must always be borne in mind that the validity of linearisation depends on the mode of use of the model. Since linearisation consists in neglecting all but the linear terms in a Taylor expansion, it is necessary to be sure that such neglection will not cause serious error. It is not difficult to put an upper bound on the error caused by linearisation, once the usage of the model has been defined. It is the magnitude of the deviation of the solution from the solution $x_s(t)$ (about which linearisation has taken place) together with the form of the non-linearity that determine the accuracy obtainable from a linear model of a non-linear process.

It is often the case when modelling a batch process that a linearised model will suffice to describe the operation except in the start-up and shut-down stages of the process.

An example of linearisation can be found in Appendix B.

8.2 Linearity in parameters

When a system model is said to be linear or non-linear the statement refers by tradition to the relation between input and output variables. This classification coincides completely with the classification of differential equations into linear and non-linear. The further property of a model being linear in the parameters is important in modelling.

The two properties (linear in the usual sense and linear in the parameters) are independent.

Let y be the output of the process and let $\hat{y}$ be the output of a process model. Let a_i, $i = 1, \ldots, n$ be the parameters of the model.

The model is said to be *linear in the parameters* if the error e between model and process is linear in each of the a_i. For instance, if e is defined as the difference between actual and predicted output, then for the model to be linear in the parameters, we must have

$$e = \|y - \hat{y}\| = \Sigma \, \alpha_i a_i \quad \text{for some scalars } \alpha_i, \quad i = 1, \ldots, n.$$

Where the model is linear in the parameters, certain types of parameter estimation techniques, such as linear regression, may be applicable. It should be noted, however, that the property of being linear in the parameters is not an intrinsic property of the model only, since it also depends on how the error e between model and process is defined.

For instance, if the model of a single-output system is a linear differential equation

$$(D^n + a_{n-1}D^{n-1} + \ldots + a_0)\hat{y} = u, \tag{8.2.1}$$

where $D = d/dt$, and the error is defined $e = y - \hat{y}$. Then

$$e = y - \frac{u}{D^n + a_{n-1}D^{n-1} + \ldots , + a_0} \tag{8.2.2}$$

and it is evident that e is not linear in the parameters a_i.

However, if with the same model we define the error by

$$e = (D^n + a_{n-1}D^{n-1} + \ldots + a_0)y - u \tag{8.2.3}$$

then e is now linear in the parameters.

A discussion of the definition of model error was given in Chapter 3, Section 3.

Chapter 9

Model reduction techniques

9.0 Introduction

Given a large linear dynamic model, reduction techniques allow the systematic derivation of a reduced order model whose behaviour approximates that of the original model.

Two methods, due to Davison[1] and Marshall[2] are described below. Both depend on eigenvalue analysis.

The method of principal component analysis is a classical technique of statistics for model reduction. It bears a resemblance to Davison's method and is described in Appendix A.

9.1 Davison's method[1] for model reduction

9.1.1 Principle
Let the *original system* of order n be represented by the equation

$$\dot{x}(t) = Ax(t) + Bu(t). \tag{9.1.1}$$

A new *reduced system* of specified order l

$$\dot{y}(t) = Gy(t) + Hu(t) \tag{9.1.2}$$

is to be constructed approximating the original system.

In the approximation, eigenvalues of large absolute value are neglected. Let the eigenvalues of the matrix A be arranged in ascending order of absolute value.

$$\{\lambda_1, \lambda_2, ..., \lambda_l, ..., \lambda_n\}.$$

Denote the set of ordered eigenvalues by Γ.

The matrix G is required to have the eigenvalues $\{\lambda_1, \lambda_2, ..., \lambda_l\}$ and the eigenvectors of G must be a best approximation (in a sense explained below) to the eigenvectors of A.

In Davison's method, the matrix G is found by decomposing the time response of the original system and selecting for inclusion in the reduced model, only those terms that involve the first l eigenvalues in the set Γ.

A certain degree of judgement needs to be exercised at the stage where eigenvalues have to be chosen for the reduced model — there being both mathematical and physical conditions to be satisfied.

9.1.2 The method

Assume that the initial condition $x(0)$ is zero and that $Bu(t)$ satisfies

$$Bu(t) = 0, \quad t < 0,$$

$$Bu(t) = b, \quad t \geqslant 0.$$

Assume also that the eigenvalues of A are real and distinct (in fact the method holds for complex or repeated eigenvalues provided that the eigenvectors of A are not degenerate).

Denote by Λ the diagonal matrix of eigenvalues and by E the modal matrix

$$[\alpha^1 \mathbin{\vert} \alpha^2 \mathbin{\vert} \ldots \mathbin{\vert} \alpha^n] \quad \text{of eigenvectors.}$$

Then

$$\Phi(t) = E \exp(\Lambda t) E^{-1}.$$

The solution of eqn. (9.1.1) under the conditions assumed is

$$x(t) = \int_0^t \Phi(t - \tau) b \, d\tau$$

$$= \int_0^t E \exp(\Lambda(t - \tau)) E^{-1} b \, d\tau, \tag{9.1.3}$$

which on integrating becomes

$$x(t) = E \begin{pmatrix} \dfrac{e^{\lambda_1 t} - 1}{\lambda_1} & 0 \\ 0 & \dfrac{e^{\lambda_n \tau} - 1}{\lambda_n} \end{pmatrix} E^{-1} b. \tag{9.1.4}$$

Let the ith row of the matrix E^{-1} be denoted β^i then in expanded form

$$\begin{pmatrix} x_1 \\ \vdots \\ x_n \end{pmatrix} = \left(\frac{e^{\lambda_1 t} - 1}{\lambda_1} \right) \alpha^1 (\beta^1)^T b + \ldots + \left(\frac{e^{\lambda_n t} - 1}{\lambda_n} \right) \alpha^n (\beta^n)^T b. \tag{9.1.5}$$

Using starred symbols to denote quantities relevant to the reduced system, the time solution y for the reduced system can be written

$$\begin{pmatrix} y_1 \\ \vdots \\ y_l \end{pmatrix} = \left(\frac{e^{\lambda_1^* t} - 1}{\lambda_1^*} \right) \alpha^{1^*} (\beta^{1^*})^T_b^* + \ldots + \left(\frac{e^{\lambda_l^* t} - 1}{\lambda_l^*} \right) \alpha^{l^*} (\beta^{l^*})^T b^*. \tag{9.1.6}$$

Choose next the l state variables x_i that are to be kept in the reduced model and denote the resultant l-dimensional vector by z. Denote the residual elements of x that are not included in z by v so that v is a vector of dimension $n - l$.

Consider eqn. (9.1.5) with only the first l eigenvalues of Γ retained. The response becomes

$$\begin{pmatrix} x_1 \\ \vdots \\ x_n \end{pmatrix} = \left(\frac{e^{\lambda_1 t} - 1}{\lambda_1} \right) \alpha^1 (\beta^1)^T b + \ldots + \left(\frac{e^{\lambda_l t} - 1}{\lambda_l} \right) \alpha^l (\beta^l)^T b, \qquad (9.1.7)$$

which can be written in a condensed form

$$\begin{pmatrix} x_1 \\ \vdots \\ x_n \end{pmatrix} = \xi_1 \alpha^1 + \ldots + \xi_l \alpha^l \qquad (9.1.8)$$

or

$$x = E_a \xi, \ldots,$$

where

$$\xi_i = \frac{e^{\lambda_i t} - 1}{\lambda_i} (\beta^i)^T b, \quad \xi = (\xi_1, \ldots, \xi_l)^T$$

and E_a is obtained by deletion of the appropriate columns of E. If now only the l state variables $z_1, \ldots, z_l$ are considered in eqn. (9.1.8) we can write

$$z = E_b \xi, \qquad (9.1.10)$$

where E_b is obtained from E_a by deleting the rows corresponding to elements in the v vector and including the rows corresponding to the z vector. E_b has dimension $l \times l$.

For instance let x be

$$\begin{bmatrix} x_1 \\ x_2 \\ x_3 \\ x_3 \\ x_4 \\ x_5 \\ x_6 \end{bmatrix} \quad \text{with} \quad E_a = \begin{bmatrix} e_{11} & \cdots & e_{12} \\ \cdot & \cdots & \cdot \\ \cdot & \cdots & \cdot \\ \cdot & \cdots & \cdot \\ \cdot & \cdots & \cdot \\ \cdot & \cdots & \cdot \\ e_{61} & \cdots & e_{62} \end{bmatrix}$$

Suppose $z_1 = x_2$ and $z_2 = x_5$ then

$$E_b = \begin{pmatrix} e_{21} & e_{22} \\ e_{51} & e_{52} \end{pmatrix}. \qquad (9.1.11)$$

Finally, define the $(n - l) \times l$ matrix E_c by the relation

$$v = E_c \xi. \qquad (9.1.12)$$

From eqn. (9.1.10)

$$\xi = E_b^{-1}z. \tag{9.1.13}$$

From eqns. (9.1.12) and (9.1.13)

$$v = E_c E_b^{-1}z. \tag{9.1.14}$$

x was decomposed into vectors z, v of lower dimension, hence there exists matrices A', A'' such that

$$\dot{z} = A'z + A''v, \tag{9.1.15}$$

where A', A'' are obtained by partitioning the A matrix.

From eqns. (9.1.14) and (9.1.15)

$$\dot{z} = [A' + A''E_c E_b^{-1}]z = A^*z. \tag{9.1.16}$$

The eigenvalues of A^* coincide with the first l eigenvalues in Γ and the eigenvectors are the projection, onto a subspace of reduced dimensions, of the first l eigenvectors of A. The proof of this can be taken as an exercise or can be found in the Appendix of Davisons paper.[1]

Thus, A^* is the required matrix G for eqn. (9.1.2) and the vector z is the vector y.

The elements from x for inclusion in the z vector must be chosen so that, physically, the set of state variables in the reduced model represent between them the most significant effects present in the original model. Mathematically, this corresponds to ensuring that det (E_c) is large.

The forcing matrix H is given by

$$H = E_c E_d, \tag{9.1.17}$$

where E_d is a matrix formed from the first l rows of the matrix $E^{-1}b$.

To derive this relation, equate the time solutions of eqn. (9.1.1) (the original system) and eqn. (9.1.12) (the reduced system) — neglecting modes higher than the lth. According to the paper, the H matrix so obtained is valid for any input although step inputs were assumed in the derivation.

The paper[1] contains numerical examples together with plots of comparisons of time response of original and reduced systems.

These numerical examples relate to the reduction of an original model of 9th order. However, the greatest need for model reduction is in the case where the original model has an order of several hundred. In such cases the computational problem of determining the eigenvalues/eigenvectors of the original system arises. The availability of efficient means of computing eigenvalues of large systems will be a key question in deciding whether to apply Davison's method.

9.2 Marshall's method[2]

With the same notation and assumptions as above, assume that the nth order system of eqn. (9.1.1) is to be reduced to a specified order l.

Equation (9.1) is partitioned to yield

$$\begin{pmatrix} \dot{x}^1 \\ \dot{x}^2 \end{pmatrix} = \begin{pmatrix} A_1 & A_2 \\ A_3 & A_4 \end{pmatrix} \begin{pmatrix} x^1 \\ x^2 \end{pmatrix} + \begin{pmatrix} B_1 \\ B_2 \end{pmatrix} (u), \tag{9.2.1}$$

where the partitioning is so arranged that the l state variables to be retained are in x^1.

Now put

$$x = Ez,$$

where E is the modal matrix of A. Then

$$\dot{z}(t) = \Lambda z(t) + E^{-1}Bu.$$

Partitioning leads to

$$\begin{pmatrix} \dot{z}^1 \\ \dot{z}^2 \end{pmatrix} = \begin{pmatrix} \Lambda_1 & 0 \\ 0 & \Lambda_2 \end{pmatrix} \begin{pmatrix} z^1 \\ z^2 \end{pmatrix} + \begin{pmatrix} V_1 & V_2 \\ V_3 & V_4 \end{pmatrix} \begin{pmatrix} B_1 \\ B_2 \end{pmatrix} (u), \tag{9.2.3}$$

where

$$V = \begin{pmatrix} V_1 & V_2 \\ V_3 & V_4 \end{pmatrix} = E^{-1}. \tag{9.2.4}$$

The first l eigenvalues are in Λ_1 and represent the most significant time constants of the system. The short time constants are neglected; this amounts to assuming instantaneous algebraic relations to describe these effects.

Putting $\dot{z}^2 = 0$ in eqn. (9.2.3) achieves the desired neglection and leads to

$$\dot{z}^1 = \Lambda_1 z^1 + (V_1 B_1 + V_2 B_2)u, \tag{9.2.5}$$

$$0 = \Lambda_2 z^2 + (V_3 B_1 + V_4 B_2)u. \tag{9.2.6}$$

From eqn. (9.2.2)

$$z = Vx = \begin{pmatrix} V_1 & V_2 \\ V_3 & V_4 \end{pmatrix} \begin{pmatrix} x^1 \\ x^2 \end{pmatrix}. \tag{9.2.7}$$

From eqn. (9.2.7)

$$z^2 = V_3 x^1 + V_4 x^2 = - \Lambda_2^{-1}(V_3 B_1 + V_4 B_2)u,$$

$$x^2 = - V_4^{-1}V_3 x^1 - V_4^{-1}\Lambda_2^{-1}(V_3 B_1 + V_4 B_2)u. \tag{9.2.8}$$

From eqns. (9.2.1) and (9.2.8)

$$\dot{x}^1 = (A_1 - A_2V_4^{-1}V_3)x^1 + [B_1 - A_2V_4^{-1}\Lambda_2^{-1}(V_3B_1 + V_4B_2)]u, \quad (9.2.9)$$

which is the desired reduced equation.

The remaining state variables, should they be required, can be calculated algebraically.

Marshall's method has the advantage that the steady-state solution of the reduced model is identical to that of the original (this is not true with Davison's method).

Marshall gives the following simple example in his paper. Let

$$A = \begin{pmatrix} -1 & 1 \\ 0 & -10 \end{pmatrix}, \quad B = \begin{pmatrix} 1 \\ 2 \end{pmatrix},$$

then

$$E = \begin{pmatrix} 1 & 1 \\ 0 & -9 \end{pmatrix}, \quad V = \begin{pmatrix} 0 & 1/9 \\ 0 & -1/9 \end{pmatrix}$$

Reduction of this second order system to first order results in

$$\left. \begin{array}{l} x_1 = -x_1 + (6/5)u, \\ x_2 = \quad\ (1/5)u. \end{array} \right\} \qquad (9.2.10)$$

See also Reference 3, which contains a useful computer program.

9.3 References

1 DAVISON, E. J.: 'A method for simplifying linear dynamic systems', *IEEE Trans. Auto Control*, 1966, **11**, pp. 93–101.
2 MARSHALL, S. A.: 'An approximate method for reducing the order of a linear system', *Control*, 1966, **10**, pp. 642–643.
3 ELLIS, J. E. and ROBERTS, P. D.: 'A method of order reduction and a criterion for control model adequacy in controller design', *IEE Conference Publication Number 194, 'Control and its applications'*, 1981, pp. 191–195.

Chapter 10

An introduction to integral equations

10.0 Introduction

Models of dynamical systems are normally centred around a set of differential equations. However, integral equations are in some ways more powerful mathematical tools and for certain phenomena it is natural to look to integral equation models. Functional analysis is capable of solving, in a unified manner but at an abstract level, many of the problems of systems modelling. This is particularly so in the case of distributed parameter modelling where the methods of linear algebra are no longer applicable. However, when we have a result in functional analysis terms and wish to return to a more concrete or algorithmic representation, we are led quite often to an integral equation. This is hardly surprising since much of the mathematical analysis currently in use was produced by workers such as Hilbert and Banach in abstraction and generalisation of results arising during their study of integral equations. Thus, when we wish to be concrete we have to go backwards along the stream of mathematical development from a Hilbert space representation to an integral equation.

The small book of Green[1] is recommended as an introduction and source of supplementary reading.

Let $k(x, y)$ be a function of the two real variables x, y satisfying

$$\int_a^b \int_a^b |k(x, y)|\, dx,\, dy < \infty. \tag{10.0.1}$$

If we take a function $f(y) \in L^2$ *of y* only and form the expression

$$\int_a^b k(x, y)f(y)\, dy$$

we obtain a function of x, say $g(x)$ to give the mapping $A\colon f(y) \to g(x)$.

A is an *integral operator* satisfying $Af(y)$ (both $f(y)$, $g(x)$ are members of the function space L^2). $k(x, y)$ is known as the *kernel* of the integral operator A.

10.0.1 Example

$$g(x) = \int_0^\pi \underbrace{\sin (x + y)}_{\text{kernel}} f(y)\, dy. \tag{10.0.2}$$

The kernel function $k(x, y)$ can be approximated by the nth partial sum k_n where

$$k_n(x, y) = \sum_{i=1}^{n} \sum_{i=1}^{n} k_{ij} u_i(x) \overline{v_j(y)}, \tag{10.0.3}$$

where the k_{ij} are the coefficients of k in the double Fourier series and are given by

$$k_{ij} = \int_a^b \int_a^b k(x, y) u_i(x) \overline{v_j(y)} \, dx \, dy. \tag{10.0.4}$$

The operator A can thus be approximated by substituting $k_n(x, y)$ for $k(x, y)$ so that

$$A \simeq \int_a^b k_n(x, y) f(y) \, dy$$

$$= \int_a^b \sum_{i=1}^{n} \sum_{i=1}^{n} k_{ij} u_i(x) \overline{v_j(y)} \, f(y) dy. \tag{10.0.5}$$

10.1 Integral equations

A linear operator equation of the form $(I - \lambda A)y = f$ is called an *integral equation*, usually written in the form

$$y(x) - \lambda \int_a^b k(x, t) y(t) \, dt = f(x) \tag{10.1.1}$$

under conditions of sufficient continuity. Equation (10.1.1) is called a *Fredholm equation*.

The simpler equation

$$Ay = f$$

or

$$\int_a^b k(x, t) y(t) = f(x) \tag{10.1.2}$$

is called an integral equation of the first kind.

(If the kernel is self-adjoint so that $k(x, t) = \overline{k(t, x)}$, eqn. (10.1.2) is called a *Hilbert–Schmidt equation*.)

Finally, if the kernel function $k(x, t) = 0$ for $t > x$ the upper limit of integration may be replaced by x

$$y(x) - \lambda \int_a^x k(x, t) y(t) \, dt = f(x). \tag{10.1.3}$$

Equation (10.1.3) is called a *Volterra equation*.

These classical equations have been the subject of much analysis. We shall be more interested in approximate methods of solution.

10.1.1 Fourier series
Let f be an integrable function and let $\{u_n\}$ be an infinite sequence of vectors

of unit length satisfying $\langle u_i, u_j \rangle = \delta_{ij}$ (Kronecker delta). Such a sequence is called an *orthonormal sequence*.

10.1.2 Fourier coefficients

Let $\{u_n\}$ be an orthonormal sequence in l^2 and let $f \in l^2$. The *Fourier coefficients* of f with respect to u_n are the scalars

$$f_i \overset{\triangle}{=} \langle f, u_n \rangle, \quad i = 1, 2, \ldots, \quad \text{The expression } f = \sum_{i=1}^{\infty} f_i u_i \text{ is valid}$$

provided that $\{u_n\}$ is infinitely linearly independent, i.e., such that $\langle v, u_i \rangle = 0$ for all i implies that $v = 0$.

Such a sequence is called *complete* in which case

$$\| f \|^2 = \sum_{i=1}^{\infty} |\langle f, u_i \rangle|^2 \quad \text{(Parseval's formula)}. \tag{10.1.4}$$

Given an arbitrary element in l^2, i.e., a sequence of scalars $a_1, \ldots$ This sequence may be regarded as the Fourier coefficients of a unique element in an abstract Hilbert space and conversely.

10.2 An operator on a finite dimensional space can always be represented by a matrix. Can an operator on a function space be so represented?

Let $A: H \to H'$ be an operator between two Hilbert spaces H, H' and let $\{u_j\}$, $\{v_i\}$ be orthonormal sequences for H, H' respectively.

Then $f \in H$ can be expressed

$$f = \sum_{j=1}^{\infty} f_j u_j. \tag{10.2.1}$$

Since A is linear it can be applied to each term of the Fourier series (the f are scalars) to give

$$Af = \sum_{j=1}^{\infty} f_j A u_j. \tag{10.2.2}$$

Also

$$\langle Af, v_i \rangle = \sum_{j=1}^{\infty} f_j \langle A u_j, v_i \rangle. \tag{10.2.3}$$

Let $g \in H'$, then

$$g = \sum_{i=1}^{\infty} g_i v_i, \tag{10.2.4}$$

where again the g_i are the Fourier coefficients of the function g with respect to the v_i. Thus

$$\langle Af, g \rangle = \sum_{j=1}^{\infty} f_j \langle Au_j, g \rangle$$

$$= \sum_{j} f_j \langle Au_j, \sum_{i} g_i v_i \rangle$$

$$= \sum_{j} \sum_{i} f_j \bar{g}_i \langle Au_j, v_i \rangle$$

$$= \sum_{j} \sum_{i} \bar{g}_i k_{ij} f_j. \tag{10.2.5}$$

The double series can be shown to be convergent and k can be considered as an infinite dimensional *kernel matrix*, representing A with respect to the chosen bases for H, H'.

Notice that if $\langle Au_j, v_i \rangle = \delta_{ji}$ *then the kernel matrix will be diagonal* since $k_{ij} = 0$ unless $i = j$.

If we take $\{Au_j\}$ as a basis for H', i.e., if we have $v_j = Au_j, j = 1, ..., r$, then the equation $y - Ay = f$ can be treated by the procedure below.

Taking the inner product with $u_i, i = 1, ..., r$ gives

$$\langle y, u_i \rangle = \langle f, u_i \rangle + \sum_{j=1}^{r} \langle y_j v_j, u_i \rangle \tag{10.2.6}$$

or

$$y_i = f_i + \sum_{j=1}^{r} y_j \langle v_j, u_i \rangle. \tag{10.2.7}$$

The y_i are the Fourier coefficients of y with respect to the basis $\{u_i\}$. This approach has been used in Chapter 11 as a method for the solution of a distributed parameter problem.

10.3 Validity of truncating the infinite dimensional K matrix

10.3.1 Definition
An operator A is defined to be *completely continuous* if

$$f_n \to f \Longrightarrow Af_n \to Af \quad \text{in norm.}$$

A completely continuous operator maps weakly convergent sequences into strongly convergent sequences (thus the identity operator is not completely continuous).

10.3.2 Theorem 10.3.1
Every completely continuous operator can be approximated arbitrarily closely in norm by an operator of finite rank (i.e., by a finite number of terms in the summation (10.2.5)).

From an algorithmic point of view, subject to continuity conditions on the operator A, the kernel matrix can be truncated to be of finite dimension and then the solution of the equation

$$(I - A)y = f$$

can be achieved by algebraic methods.

Let $y_j = \langle y, u_j \rangle$ be Fourier coefficients of y in H, $j = 1, ..., r$. Then $y - Ay = f$ is the same as

$$y = f + \sum_{j=1}^{r} y_j v_j. \tag{10.3.1}$$

10.3.3 Numerical solution

The methods outlined above can be mechanised with the aid of quadrature and hill climbing techniques to provide powerful general methods for the modelling of a wide class of systems.

An alternative method of solution makes use of the *Neumann series*.

Let $D = I - A$ then the Neumann series represents D^{-1} by the series

$$D^{-1} = I + A + A^2 + ..., \tag{10.3.2}$$

the series being convergent provided that

$$|\lambda_i| < 1/\|D\|, \forall i \tag{10.3.3}$$

Other methods of solution are described in Reference 1.

10.4 References

1 GREEN, C. D.: *Integral Equation Methods*, Nelson, 1965.

Chapter 11

The modelling of distributed parameter systems

11.0 Introduction

In modelling by ordinary differential equations there is an implicit assumption that all effects are concentrated at points in space. Such an assumption is always an idealisation and for many processes where spatial variation is important, a distributed parameter model is required.

Examples of distributed effects that may need to be modelled explicitly are: temperature variation in a furnace and composition variation in a reactor or in a river estuary. The modelling of distributed parameter systems remains a current research area of considerable interest. In Section 11.3 we describe an approach using functional analysis.

11.1 Modelling by partial differential equations

The most obvious approach to modelling distributed parameter systems is simply to write down the appropriate partial differential equations. However, the extensive literature on partial differential equations is mostly concerned with very well defined classical problems such as vibrating strings and heated bars. There is scarcely any information to be found on how to write down the partial differential equations representing an arbitrary complex system with distributed parameters. Thus, on many occasions it will not be possible to write down suitable partial differential equations.

Assuming that partial differential equations can be written down, there still remains the question of their numerical solution. One partial differential equation can be approximated by a set of ordinary equations — the method is illustrated sufficiently by the example below. A general form for the partial differential equation in one spatial dimension is

$$\frac{\partial x}{\partial t} + V \frac{\partial x}{\partial l} + r = 0. \tag{11.1.1}$$

x might be temperature within a moving column of liquid having velocity V in the l direction. r represents rate of heat generation in the column.

The *numerical solution of partial differential equations* requires discretisation to produce a set of ordinary differential equations that are then solved by conventional methods for such sets of equations. Consider eqn. (11.1.1) above. $\partial x/\partial l$ can be written $\partial x/\partial l$ (t, l) since it depends on both time and distance along the column. However, for a sufficiently small spatial region about a point l_i so that $l_i - \varepsilon \leqslant l \leqslant l_i + \varepsilon$, $\partial x/\partial l$ can be considered to be a function of time only. Let

$$p_i(t) = \frac{\partial x}{\partial l}(t).$$

The spatial dimensions can be split into n elements each of length 2ε, so that the set equations to be solved is

$$\frac{dx}{dt} + Vp_i(t) + r = 0, \quad i = 1, \ldots, n. \tag{11.1.2}$$

Examination of what has just been done shows that it is equivalent to the physically based assumption that the moving column can be portioned into n zones — within each zone the variation of x with l can be assumed constant at any particular time t.

The discretisation of distributed systems, which is a necessary step in their numerical solution can be undertaken on physical grounds by partitioning into spatial zones in the model formulation stage. Alternatively, discretisation can be undertaken on a purely mathematical basis at a later stage. The two approaches lead to a similar set of ordinary differential equations to be solved. However, for a complex set of partial differential equations it may not be possible, where the second approach is used, to give a physical meaning to the discretisation. As a second illustration of discretisation, consider the equation which arises in two dimensional temperature diffusion. Let $\theta =$ temperature where y, z are the two spatial dimensions.

The variable $\partial^2\theta/(\partial y, \partial z)$ can be spatially discretised as follows.

$$\frac{\partial^2\theta}{\partial y, \partial z} = \frac{\partial}{\partial y}\left(\frac{\partial\theta}{\partial z}\right) \simeq \frac{\partial}{\partial y}\left(\frac{\theta(y_0, z_0 + \varepsilon) - \theta(y_0, z_0 - \varepsilon)}{2\varepsilon}\right) \tag{11.1.3}$$

$$\simeq \left(\frac{\theta(y_0 + \varepsilon, z_0 + \varepsilon)}{2\varepsilon} - \frac{\theta(y_0 + \varepsilon, z_0 - \varepsilon)}{2\varepsilon}\right)\frac{1}{2\varepsilon}$$

$$- \left(\frac{\theta(y_0 - \varepsilon, z_0 + \varepsilon)}{2\varepsilon} - \frac{\theta(y_0 - \varepsilon, z_0 - \varepsilon)}{2\varepsilon}\right)\frac{1}{2\varepsilon}.$$

$$\tag{11.1.4}$$

Thus

$$\frac{\partial^2\theta}{\partial y,\, \partial z}\bigg|_{y_0,z_0} \simeq \frac{\theta(y_0 + \varepsilon,\, z_0 + \varepsilon) - \theta(y_0 - \varepsilon,\, z_0 + \varepsilon)}{4\varepsilon^2}$$

$$- \frac{\theta(y_0 + \varepsilon,\, z_0 - \varepsilon) - \theta(y_0 - \varepsilon,\, z_0 - \varepsilon)}{4\varepsilon^2} \tag{11.1.5}$$

This approach to the modelling of two-dimensional temperature distribution requires a spatial grid to be drawn. At each node of the grid a different ordinary differential equation needs to be solved (see Fig. 11.1).

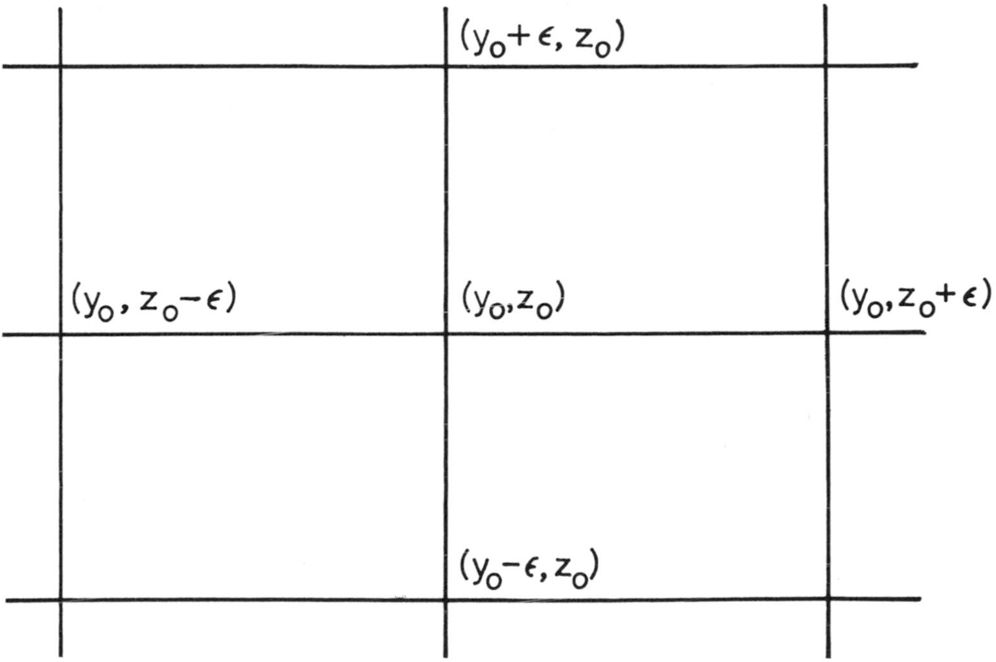

Fig. 11.1 *Spatial discretisation of a partial differential equation*

The modelling of distributed systems is in practice very difficult. Discretisation can produce misleading spurious effects in the model, due to the artificial discontinuities that are introduced at the boundary of spatial zones. In some applications, such as the modelling of melting and solidification, the spatial boundary is changing with time so that the discretisation grid may have to be expanded as the solution proceeds.

Reference 1 is concerned particularly with the numerical solution of partial differential equations.

11.2 Modelling by explicit spatial discretisation

By spatial discretisation we mean the slicing of a physical model into n spatial zones. The zones are small enough to allow conditions within each to be regarded as spatially uniform, hence the effects can be lumped and the system represented by n sets of ordinary differential equations which are solved in the usual way. For instance, assume that a travelling load continuous furnace is to be modelled.

The furnace can be sliced into n zones as shown in Fig. 11.2. In each zone the temperature is assumed constant.

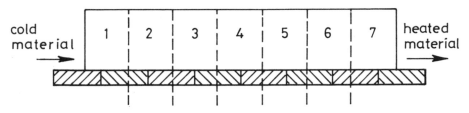

Fig. 11.2 *Schematic diagram of travelling load furnace*

This type of approach is often used successfully but there are a number of problems that can occur. Two of these are:

(*a*) The discretisation introduces discontinuities in the derivatives of the variables being modelled. When the model is used, spurious behaviour having no counterpart in the physical system may be generated in the model.
(*b*) There are logistic difficulties in organising the model. Considering the diagram above, the material to be heated varies in dimensions so that it does not move neatly from zone-to-zone.

A model based on spatial discretisation is suitable only for generating numerical results and cannot easily be used in any analytical manner.

11.3 An approach using functional analysis

Let Σ represent a distributed parameter system to be modelled.

Define $x(t, z)$ to be the system state and $u(t, z)$ to be the system input. t, $z \in R^1$, where t corresponds to time and z corresponds to a spatial variable. $x \in X$, $u \in U$; U and X being spaces of Lebesgue integrable functions. Assume that the system Σ is linear and time invariant.

Then, just as for linear multivariable systems we can write

$$\dot{x}(t) = Ax(t) + Bu(t), \tag{11.3.1}$$

where $A: X \to X$, $B: U \to X$ are linear operators that are in general unbounded.

This is a much more generalised situation than in the usual linear multivariable case. u and x are functions rather than vectors, the state space is infinite dimensional and the operators A, B are unbounded and not representable by matrices.

However, a solution of eqn. (11.3.1) can be obtained in the form

$$x(t) = T(t - t_0)x_0 + \int_{t_0}^{t} T(t - \tau)Bu(\tau)\, d\tau \tag{11.3.2}$$

where T is a transformation semi-group that is a generalisation of the transition matrix Φ for linear multivariable systems.

T is required to obey the relations:

(a) $T(t_0 - t_0) = I$ (the identity operator);
(b) $T(t_2 - t_1)T(t_1 - t_0) = T(t_2 - t_0)$, $t_2 \geqslant t_1 \geqslant t_0$ (associative property);
(c) $T(t)$ shall be bounded for all $t \geqslant 0$;
(d) $\lim_{t \to t_0} \|T(t)x - T(t_0)x\| = 0$, $x \in X$, (strong continuity).

The relations (a) to (d) can be derived from the usual axioms that a well-posed dynamical system must obey. Taken together they require that T should be a *strongly continuous semi-group*.

Questions of immediate interest concern the relation between the operator A of eqn. (11.3.1) and the operator T; the relation can be summarised:

A necessary condition that the operator T be a member of a strongly continuous semi-group is that the operator A should be the *infinitesimal generator* of T.

In order for this to be achieved, two necessary conditions on A are:

(a) A must be a closed operator,
(b) the domain $D(A)$ of A must be dense in X.

Thus, from (a) although the operator A can be unbounded (since A is a partial differential operator it will often be unbounded in practice), it must be a closed operator.

Condition (b) means that any element in X can be approximated arbitrarily closely by elements in $D(A)$.

For development of *constructive methods by which T can be characterised* in terms of A we note that

$$T(t) = \mathcal{L}^{-1}\{R(s, A)\}, \tag{11.3.3}$$

where L is the Laplace operator.

$R(S, A)$ is the resolvent of $A = (SI - A)^{-1}$.

Hence a time solution of eqn. (11.3.1) is possible by taking the inverse Laplace transform of the resolvent of the operator A.

Notice that this is exactly analogous to the relation for linear multivariable systems in terms of matrices

$$\Phi(t) = \mathcal{L}^{-1}\{(sI - A)^{-1}\}. \tag{11.3.4}$$

Alternatively, $T(t)$ can be defined by the relation

$$Ax = \lim_{h \to 0} \frac{T(h) - I}{h} x; \quad \forall x \ \varepsilon \ D(A). \tag{11.3.5}$$

Methods of generating the operator T have been given in Dunford and Schwartz[2] and in Balakrishnan[3] while an application to river modelling has been described in Hullett.[4] It must be pointed out that the integral in eqn. (11.3.2) needs interpreting with care since the integrand takes values in a Banach space. The integral is to be interpreted as a Bôchner integral which is a suitable generalisation of the Lebesgue integral.

$T(t)$, generated as above, maps the state function $x(0, z)$ into the state function $x(t, z)$. A more practical approach relies on approximating the function x as a linear combination of a finite number of orthogonal basis functions. The operator A can be represented as a finite matrix and a numerically tractable approach can be developed.

The approach is simplest when X is the Hilbert space L^2 since then the element x can be approximated arbitrarily closely by an element in the sequence space l^2. This sequence can be truncated to obtain whatever accuracy is required and the development is as shown below.

Let x belong to the Hilbert space $X = L^2(a, b)$ and let $\{\gamma_i\}$ be an orthonormal basis for X.

Let $x_i = \langle x, \gamma_i \rangle \gamma$ so that $x = \Sigma_i x_i \gamma_i$. $x(z)$ is the state of the system with $z \ \epsilon \ (a, b)$ and x can be expressed

$$x(z) = \sum_{s=1}^{\infty} x_i \gamma_i.$$

This leads to the equation

$$\begin{pmatrix} \dot{x}_1 \\ \dot{x}_2 \\ \vdots \\ \dot{x}_r \end{pmatrix} = \begin{pmatrix} A \end{pmatrix} \begin{pmatrix} x_1 \\ x_2 \\ \vdots \\ x_r \end{pmatrix} + \begin{pmatrix} B \end{pmatrix} \begin{pmatrix} u_1 \\ u_2 \\ \vdots \\ u_m \end{pmatrix}, \tag{11.3.6}$$

where r is an integer high enough to give sufficient accuracy. Equation (11.3.6) can be solved by the usual methods of linear multivariable theory.

An alternative approach that would allow more generalised effects to be represented may be to use an integral equation representation. Assume a single input $u(t)$ is applied over the time interval $(0, T)$ with $u(t) \in U$ is the Hilbert space $L^2(0, T)$.

Let (ζ_j) be an orthonormal basis for U.

Define $u_j = \langle u, \zeta_j \rangle$, so that $u = \Sigma_j u_j \zeta_j$.

A very general model can be postulated as $x(z) = Eu(t)$ where E is a general operator. Thus

$$x = E \, \Sigma_j u_j, \quad \zeta_j = \Sigma_j u_j E \zeta_j; \quad E: U \to X.$$

Taking inner products with ζ_i

$$\langle x, \zeta_i \rangle = \langle \Sigma_j u_j E \zeta_j, \gamma_i \rangle$$

or

$$x_i = \Sigma_j u_j \langle E \, \zeta_j, \gamma_i \rangle$$

or

$$x = \Sigma_i x_i \gamma_i = \Sigma_i \Sigma_j u_j \langle E \zeta_j, \gamma_i \rangle \gamma_i.$$

$\langle E \zeta_j, \gamma_i \rangle$ are scalars that can be denoted c_{ji} then

$$x = \Sigma_i \Sigma_j u_j c_{ji} \, \gamma_i. \tag{11.3.7}$$

This form of model has been found valuable[5] in representing industrial distributed parameter processes.

11.4 References

The semi group approach has been pioneered principally by Balakrishnan[3,6]. Adequate mathematical support can be found in the works by Yosida[7], Dunford and Schwartz[2] and Hille and Phillips[8]. These are graduate level texts and a good background in analysis is needed for their successful use. Reference 9 covers a reduced volume of material at a more introductory level suitable for graduate engineers.

1 AMES, W. F.: *Numerical Methods for Partial Differential Equations*, Nelson, 1969.

2 DUNFORD, N. and SCHWARTZ, J. T.: *Linear operators*, Part 1, Wiley Interscience, New York, 1957.

3 BALAKRISHNAN, A. V.: 'Semi-group theory and control theory', *Proc. IFIP Congress*, 1965, pp. 157–163, Spartan Books, Washington DC, 1965.

4 HULLETT, W.: 'Optimal estuary aeration', *Appl. Math. and Optimisation*, 1974, **1**, No. 1, pp. 20–63.

5 LAU, C. C. and LEIGH, J. R.: 'Modelling of an industrial distributed parameter process'. *Proc. 5th IFAC Symposium on Identification and System Parameter Estimation*, Darmstadt, Germany, 24–28 September 1979, Publ. Pergamon Press, Paper A4.4, 1980.

6 BALAKRISHNAN, A. V.: *Applied Functional Analysis*, Springer-Verlag, Berlin, 1976.

7 YOSIDA, K.: *Functional Analysis*, Springer-Verlag, Berlin 1974.

8 HILLE, E. and PHILLIPS, R. S.: *Functional Analysis and Semi-groups*, American Mathematical Society, 1957.

9 LEIGH, J. R.: 'Functional analysis and linear control theory, Volume 156 in the series *Mathematics in Science and Engineering*, Academic Press, New York, 1980.

A review of statistical techniques

Since modelling involves the interpretation of experimental data, a knowledge of basic statistical methods is a pre-requisite for successful modelling. In particular, *planning of experiments* and *tests of significance* are topics of importance that can be pursued in many standard texts. Below is a brief review of other statistical methods for use in modelling.

A.1 Scaling of variables

It is good practice to scale variables so that they have zero mean and unity variance. In statistics this is referred to as *zero–one normalisation*.

Given a set of measurements $\{x_i\}$, $i = 1, ..., n$ the zero–one normalised variable is given by:

(*a*) subtracting the mean

$$\frac{1}{n} \sum_{i=1}^{n} x_i$$

from each measurement;
(*b*) dividing each measurement by the variance.

If $\{y_i\}$ are the normalised variables then

$$y_i = \frac{x_i - \dfrac{1}{n} \sum_{i=1}^{n} x_i}{\left[\dfrac{1}{n-1} \sum_{i=1}^{n} \left(x_i - \dfrac{1}{n} \sum_{i=1}^{n} x_i \right)^2 \right]^{1/2}}. \tag{A1.1}$$

A.2 Covariance and correlation

Let $\{x_i\}$ and $\{y_i\}$ be two zero–one normalised time series. Thus, the *covariance* between x and y is defined by

$$\text{cov } (x, y) = \frac{1}{n} \sum_{i=0}^{n} x_i y_i. \qquad (A.2.1)$$

The correlation coefficient between x and y is defined by

$$R(x, y) = \text{cov } (x, y)/(\sigma^2(x) \, \sigma^2(y)), \qquad (A2.2)$$

where $\sigma^2(x)$, $\sigma^2(y)$ indicate the variances of the time series $\{x_i\}$, $\{y_i\}$.

A.2.1 Modelling by correlation techniques

This topic is covered very briefly here since there are many excellent texts covering the theory and its application.

The *auto-correlation function* of a function of time $x(t)$ is defined

$$R_{xx}(\tau) = \frac{1}{2T} \int_{-T}^{T} x(t + \tau)x(t) \, dt, \quad T \to \infty \qquad (A.2.3)$$

and the *cross-correlation function* between two functions of time is defined

$$R_{xy}(\tau) = \frac{1}{2T} \int_{-T}^{T} x(t + \tau)x(t) \, dt, \quad T \to \infty. \qquad (A.2.4)$$

The *spectral density* $S(w)$ is defined

$$S(w) = \int_{-\infty}^{\infty} R(\tau) \, e^{-j\omega\tau} \, d\tau. \qquad (A.2.5)$$

It should be noted that the auto- and cross-correlation functions are functions of the time shift τ. The spectral density is the Fourier transform of the correlation function and is a function of frequency w.

The correlation function and spectral density form a Fourier transform pair that is in many ways analogous to the impulse response, transfer function pair.

In experimental modelling of a single-input–single-output linear process with input u and output y, the auto-correlation function $R_{uu}(\tau)$ and the cross-correlation function $R_{uy}(\tau)$ are determined, often by a special purpose correlator.

Let the system inpulse response be $h(t)$ then the relation between $R_{uu}(\tau)$, $R_{uy}(\tau)$ is

$$R_{uy}(\tau) = \int_{-\infty}^{\infty} R_{uu}(\tau - \alpha)h(\alpha) \, d\alpha. \qquad (A.2.6)$$

Then, Fourier transforming

$$S_{uy}(w) = G(w)S_{uu}(w), \qquad (A.2.7)$$

where $G(w)$ is the system transfer function.

Since both $S_{uu}(w)$, $S_{uy}(w)$ can be determined experimentally for instance by fast Fourier transform, the system transfer function $G(w)$ can be determined numerically.

In application of this technique, attention must be devoted to the nature and magnitude of the input test signal and the length of time over which the identification experiment is to run.

A.3 Regression models

A regression model is most easily applied to a linear non-dynamic multi-input single output model of the form

$$y = \sum_{i=1}^{k} a_i u_i. \tag{A.3.1}$$

Given n measurement sets of the y and u values, dennote these by $\hat{y}_j$ and $\hat{u}_{ij}$ respectively, where $i = 1, ..., k, j = 1, ..., n$. The sets of data can be written $[\hat{y} \mid \hat{U}]$ where $\hat{y}$ is a k vector and $\hat{U}$ is an $n \times k$ matrix.

Regression analysis consists in choosing parameters $\hat{a}_i, i = 1, ..., k$ such that a best fit in some sense is obtained between process and model. The assumptions most commonly made in regression analysis are:

(*a*) the measurements u are not subject to error (thus the superscript can be dropped);
(*b*) the errors $y_j - \hat{y}_j$ are randomly distributed with a normal distribution and the errors are statistically independent.

Usually the $\hat{a}_i, i = 1, ..., k$ will be chosen to minimise the criterion

$$J = \sum_{j=1}^{n} (y_j - \hat{y}_j)^2.$$

Substituting for y_j and setting $\partial J / \partial a_i = 0$ for $i = 1, ..., k$ yields the relation

$$U^T U \hat{a} = U^T y, \tag{A.3.2}$$

$$\hat{a} = (U^T U)^{-1} U^T y. \tag{A.3.3}$$

Equation (A3.3) can be visualised geometrically as an application of the projection theorem — see Fig. A.1.
$\hat{y} \in E_1$, the n-dimensional observation space.
$y \in E_2$, the k-dimensional modelling space.
By the projection theorem, $\hat{y} - y$ must be orthogonal to every element u in E_2.

Thus, the inner product

$$\langle \hat{y} - y, u \rangle = 0, \qquad \forall u \in E_2,$$

or

$$\langle \hat{y}, u \rangle - < y, u > = 0, \qquad \forall u \in E_2.$$

ω = angular velocity of motor

J = mechanical inertia of armature and load

F = viscous friction coefficient

k_1 is a constant

$f(I_f)$ is the nonlinear expression relating Φ with I_f.

By substitution we obtain two differential equations

$$\dot{I_f} = \frac{1}{L_f}(V_f - I_f R_f),$$

$$\dot{\omega} = \frac{1}{J}(k_1 k_2 I_f\left(\frac{V_a - k_1 f(I_f)\omega}{R_a}\right) - F\omega). \tag{B.2}$$

Linearisation of the equations

Put

$$\left.\begin{aligned}
V_f &= U_1 + u_1 \\
V_a &= U_2 + u_2 \\
I_f &= X_1 + x_1 \\
\omega &= X_2 + x_2
\end{aligned}\right\} \tag{B.3}$$

$$\frac{df(I_f)}{dx_1}\bigg|_{I_f=X_1} = k_2, \quad \text{where } k_2 \text{ is a constant.}$$

Then eqns. (B1) and (B2) can be written in the linearised form

$$\left.\begin{aligned}
\dot{x_1} &= a_{11}x_1 + b_{11}u_1, \\
\dot{x_2} &= a_{21}x_1 + a_{22}x_2 + b_{22}u_2,
\end{aligned}\right\} \tag{B.4}$$

where

$$a_{11} = -R_f/L_f,$$

$$b_{11} = 1/L_f,$$

$$a_{21} = \frac{k_1 k_2 U_2}{JR_a} - \frac{2k_1^2 k_2 f(x_1)x_2}{R_a}$$

$$a_{22} = -\frac{1}{J}\left(\frac{k_1^2 f(x_1)^2 + F}{R_a}\right), \tag{B.5}$$

$$b_{22} = \frac{k_1 f(x_1)}{JR_a}$$

Equations (B.4) represent a linear model of the machine in the required form

$$\dot{x} = Ax + Bu. \tag{B.6}$$

General references

ABBOT, M. B.: 'Commercial and scientific aspects of applied mathematical modelling', *Adv. Eng. Software (GB)*, 1979, **1**, No. 4, pp. 147–152.

ANDREWS, J. A. and McLONE, R. R.: *Mathematical Modelling*, Butterworths, Boston, U.S.A., 1976.

ARIS, R.: *Mathematical Modelling Techiniques*, Pitman, 1978.

ATTIR, U. and DEN, M. M.: 'Dynamics and control of the activated sludge wastewater process', *Joint Automatic Control Conference*, Part III, IEEE, 1977, pp. 1185–1190.

BARNARD, B. W. and DRANSFIELD, P.: 'Predicting response of a proposed hydraulic control system using bond graphs', *Trans. ASME*, Ser. G, 1977, **99**, No.1, pp. 1–8.

BELLMAN, R. and LEE, E. S.: 'Modelling and optimisation in energy systems. I. Coal gasification modelling', *Houston J. Math. (U.S.A.)*, 1976, **2**, No. 3, pp. 329–344.

BENDER, E. A.: *An Introduction to Mathematical Modelling*, John Wiley, New York, 1978.

BEVERIDGE, G. S. C. and SCHECHTER, R. J.: *Optimisation — Theory and Practice*, McGraw-Hill, New York 1970. (The book contains a section on modelling and a comprehensive treatment of parameter estimation.)

BOYCE, W. E.: *Case Studies in Mathematical Modelling*, Pitman, 1981.

CLOSE, C. M. and FREDERICK, D. K.: *Modelling and Analysis of Dynamic Systems*, Houghton Mifflin, Boston, U.S.A., 1978.

CHIU, G. K.: 'Heat transfer and temperature control in an annealing lehr for float glass', *J. Am. Ceram. Soc., U.S.A.*, 1977, **60**, No. 11–12, pp. 477–484.

DASH, I. R. and ROSE, E.: 'Models for studying control of an iron ore sintering process', *Conf. Measurement and Control in the Handling and Processing of Material*, London, 26–27 April 1978, pp. 106–112.

EISENBERGER, G.: 'Modelling and model reduction for chemical engineering processes'. *Interkama Congress 1978*, Springer Verlag, Berlin, 1978. (In German.)

FERMELIA, A.: 'Development of helicopter flight path models', *IEEE Trans. Aerosp. and Electron Systems*, 1976, AES **12**, No. 6, pp. 783–792.

GILLMAN, D. K.: 'The application of transfer function techniques to modelling of ship control and navigation systems', *J. Navig. (GB)*, 1979, **32**, No 2, pp. 200–209.

GOLDEN, H. J.: *Mathematical Modelling of Biological Systems*, John Wiley, New York, 1977.

HABERMAN, R.: *Mathematical Models*, Prentice-Hall, Englewood Cliffs, U.S.A., 1977.

HARTLEY, M. G. (ed.), *Digital Simulation Methods*, IEE Monograph, Peter Peregrinus, 1975.

HIRATOR, H. and FUKAO, T.: 'A model of mass and energy flow in ecosystems', *Math. Biosci., U.S.A.*, 1977, **33**, No. 3–4, pp. 321–334.

HYVARINEN, L.: *Mathematical Modelling for Industrial Processes*, Springer, Berlin, 1970.

JACOBY, S. L. S. and KOWALIK, J. S.: *Mathematical Modelling with Computers*, Prentice-Hall, Englewood Cliffs, U.S.A., 1980.

JAMES, A. (ed.), *Mathematical Models in Water Pollution Control*, John Wiley, New York, 1978.

JUTAN, A., TREMBLAY, J. P., MACGREGOR, J. F. and WRIGHT, J. D.: 'Multivariable computer control of a butane hydrogenolysis reactor. I. State space reactor modelling', *AICH E J. (U.S.A.)*, 1977, **23**, No. 5, pp. 732–742.

KARNOPP, D., ROSENBERG, R. C. and VAN DIXHOORN, J. J.: *Bond Graph Techniques for Dynamic Systems in Engineering and Biology*, McGraw-Hill Book Co, New York, 1979.

KASHYAP, R. L. and RAO, A. R.: *Dynamic Stochastic Models from Empirical Data*, Academic Press, New York, 1976.

KOGAN, B. YA.: 'Modelling techniques in scientific research': *Autom. and Remote Control (U.S.A.)*, 1979, **40**, No. 6, Part 2, pp. 917–924.

KWATNEY, H. G. and KONOPACKI, W. A.: 'The modelling of a once-through steam generator for system dynamics and control studies', *1977 Joint Automatic Control Conference*, Part I, IEEE, 1977, pp. 323–331.

LEE, T. H., ADAMS, G. E. and GAINES, W. M.: *Computer Process Control — Modelling and Optimisation*, John Wiley, New York, 1968.

LEMAITRE, A., PERRON, M. and FOULARD, C.:'Modelling and parameter estimation of paper machine drying sections', *Digital Computer Applications to Process Control*, North Holland Publishing Co, Amsterdam, 1977, pp. 357–365.

LIN, S. H.: 'Two mathematical models for energy forecasting', *Int. J. Syst. Sci., GB*, 1978, **9**, No. 8, pp. 865–872.

LUCKERS, J., NILLES, P. and POOS, A., 'Modelling and control applications in the steel industry', *Proc. 6th World Congress of the Federation of Automatic Control, Pittsburgh, U.S.A.*, 30th August 1973, pp. 53.1–53.9.

MAEDA, T., NACHTIGAL, C. L. and COOK, R.: 'Mathematical models for ingot processing and control', *1977 Joint Automatic Control Conference*, Part II, San Francisco, California, U.S,A., IEEE, 1979, pp. 1713–1720.

MAHMOUD, M. S. and SINGH, M. G.: *Large Scale Systems Modelling*, Pergamon Press, New York, 1981.

McCLAMROCK, N. H.: *State Models of Dynamic Systems*, Springer, Berlin, 1980. (An introductory book with many simple examples.)

Modelling and Simulation in Practice, Pentech, GB, 1979.

NASH, P. (ed.): *Systems Modelling and Optimisation*, IEE Control Engineering Series, No. 1, Peter Peregrinus Ltd., 1981.

NICHOLSON, H. (ed.): *Modelling of Dynamical Systems*, Volumes 1 and 2, Peter Peregrinus Ltd., 1980/1981. (The two volumes contain detailed case histories.)

PENTEGOV, I. V.: 'A mathematical model of the column of a dynamic electric arc', *Autom. Weld. (GB)*, 1976, **29**, No. 6, pp. 6–10.

ROSENBROCK, H. H. and STOREY, C.: *Computational Techniques for Chemical Engineers*. Pergamon Press, New York, 1966. (A good reference having an algorithmic approach to modelling problems.)

SALID, S., JENSSON, N. A., LINDSTAD, T. and KOLBEINSEN, L.: 'Modelling, identification and control of a fluidised bed reactor', Preprints of the *5th IFAC Symposium on Identification and System Parameter Estimation*, Darmstadt, 24–28 September, 1979, pp. 907–916.

SHIBATA, C., SATO, S. and YANAGISAWA, T.: 'Dynamic models and automatic control systems for steam power plants', *Toshiba Rev. (Int. Ed.), Japan*, 1977, No. 1–7, pp. 10–14.

SHANMUNGAM, K. S.: 'An iterative procedure for obtaining reduced order system model from amplitude response data', *Modelling and Simulation*, 1976, **7**, Part II, pp. 751–755.

SMITH, J. M.: *Mathematical Modelling and Digital Simulation for Engineers and Scientists*, John Wiley, New York, 1976.

TATNALL, M. L.: 'Dynamic modelling of a gas pressure regulator for low pressure service', *Measurement and Control, GB*, 1978, **11**, No. 4, pp. 147–153.

TONG, R. M.: 'The evaluation of fuzzy models derived from experimental data', *Fuzzy Sets and Systems (Netherlands)*, 1980, **4**, No. 1, pp. 1–12.

TYSSO, A.: 'Modelling and parameter estimation of ship boilers', Preprints of the *5th IFAC Symposium on Identification and System Parameter Estimation*, Darmstadt, 24–28 Sept. 1979, pp. 949–960.

VILENIUS, M. J.: 'Dynamics of an electrohydraulic stepping motor', *Trans. ASME Ser. G*, 1977, **99**, No. 1, pp. 63–65.

WELLSTEAD, P. E.: *Introduction to Physical System Modelling*, Academic Press, New York, 1979.

WENIGER, J.: 'Thermal considerations in modelling the Linz–Donau process', *Conf. on Computer Applications in the Steel Industry*, Laxenburg, Austria, 9–11 May 1977, pp. 35–53.

WORSOE-SCHMIDT, P. and HOGAARD-KNUDSEN, H. J.: 'Thermal modelling of heat exchangers for simulation purposes', *Proc. 1976 Heat Transfer and Fluid*, Mechanics Institute, Calif., U.S.A., 21–23 June 1976, Stanford U. Press, 1976, pp. 495–521.

ZIEGLER, B.: *Theory of Modelling and Simulation*, John Wiley, New York, 1976.

Glossary of symbols

E_n	Real n dimensional space
I	The identity operator or identity matrix
L^p	The space of functions whose pth power is Lebesgue integrable
l^p	The space of sequences whose pth power is summable
s	The complex variable of Laplace transformation
$L(\ )$	Laplace transformation
Φ	The transition matrix
$\pi(\ )_i = (\ )_1 \times (\ )_2 \times (\ )_3 \times \ldots$	
$(\ )^T$	Transpose
$\overline{(\ )}$	Adjoint, complex conjugate or mean value
$\triangleq$	Equal to by definition
$<\ ,\ >$	Inner product
$\Longmapsto$	Implies
$f_n \to f$	The sequence of functions $\{f_n\}$ converges to the function f
$(\dot{\ })$	$\dfrac{d(\ )}{dt}$
$\| \ \|$	Absolute value
∇x	The gradient of x
$\| \ \|$	Norm
$\forall$	For all, for every

Index